D0425642

This book makes me want to get up and do something. Now. Today.

—**Dr. Kevin Leman,** author of *Have a New Kid by Friday* and *Have a New Husband by Friday*

This book is not only inspiring and thoughtful, but it's a profound challenge to each of us to stop focusing on what we can't do and invest our lives and energies in what we can. *She Did What She Could* is empowering to anyone who has ever asked, "What difference could I possibly make?"

—**Margaret Feinberg,** national speaker and author of *The Sacred Echo* and *Scouting the Divine*

Elisa Morgan has been unleashing power in people for a long time. This book is a little time bomb that will go off when you know your gifts and your limits and say yes to God in the midst of them.

—**John Ortberg,** pastor of Menlo Park Presbyterian Church and author of *Faith and Doubt*

I loved *She Did What She Could!* What is amazing to me is that one little phrase issues such a profound challenge for the heart and at the same time gives a deep and abiding peace. Thank you, Elisa, for this beautiful Bible teaching and the tender stories that call me to live a great big life, doing what I can today and believing God for what I can do tomorrow.

—**Angela Thomas,** speaker and best-selling author of *Do You Think I'm Beautiful?*

What an empowering book! *She Did What She Could* made me yearn for a deeper, more loving relationship with Jesus. It caused me to take a hard look at what I can do—me, an ordinary woman, profoundly and passionately loved, and to act out of that love. Simply, with a sincere heart. Not to be seen, not out of duty, obligation, or guilt, but to please and serve the One who loved me first. I want to "live loved."

—**Fern Nichols,** founder and president of Moms In Touch International

Elisa Morgan paints a vigorous picture of life on the front lines. This book is a convincing reminder that we all have Kingdom work to do, that the opportunities are all around us, that God is powerfully accomplishing his purposes for the world through us, and that more—much more!—will be accomplished when his sons and daughters serve him together.

—**Carolyn Custis James,** president of Synergy Women's Network, Inc., and author of *The Gospel of Ruth*

I love this book because it challenged me in such a way that I am now compelled to respond. And really, isn't that what we all want in a book? Elisa brilliantly weaves truths from biblical examples into our modern-day opportunities and spurs us on to action. It brings me great joy to recommend this amazing book.

—**Lysa TerKeurst,** speaker, president of Proverbs 31 Ministries and author of *Becoming More Than a Good Bible Study Girl*

She
Did
What
She
Could

She Did What She Could

Five words of Jesus that will change your life

Elisa Morgan

Tyndale House Publishers, Inc.

Carol Stream, Illinois

Visit Tyndale online at www.tyndale.com.

TYNDALE and Tyndale's quill logo are registered trademarks of Tyndale House Publishers, Inc.

She Did What She Could: Five Words of Jesus That Will Change Your Life

Copyright © 2009 by Elisa Morgan. All rights reserved.

Cover photo of jar copyright © by Imagestate/photolibrary. All rights reserved.

Cover photo of oil copyright © by ilker canikligil/iStockphoto. All rights reserved.

Cover background photo copyright © by Jacom Stephens/iStockphoto. All rights reserved.

Designed by Jacqueline L. Nuñez

Edited by Susan Taylor

Published in association with the literary agency of Alive Communications, Inc., 7680 Goddard Street, Suite 200, Colorado Springs, CO 80920, www.alivecommunications.com.

Scripture quotations are taken from the *Holy Bible*, New Living Translation, copyright © 1996, 2004, 2007 by Tyndale House Foundation. Used by permission of Tyndale House Publishers, Inc., Carol Stream, Illinois 60188. All rights reserved.

Library of Congress Cataloging-in-Publication Data

Morgan, Elisa, date.
  She did what she could (SDWSC) : five words of Jesus that will change your life / Elisa Morgan.
    p. cm.
  Includes bibliographical references.
  ISBN 978-1-4143-3378-6 (hc)
1. Christian women—Religious life. 2. Social justice—Religious aspects—Christianity. 3. Mary, of Bethany, Saint. 4. Bible. N.T. Mark XIV, 3-9—Criticism, interpretation, etc. I. Title.
  BV4527.M635 2009
  241'.677—dc22   2009022879

Printed in the United States of America

18 17 16 15 14
13 12 11 10   9   8

To the Marys.
You have each shaped my "she."

Contents

Acknowledgments

She Did What She Could came to me in a gradual, reverberating ripple until its message lodged itself solidly in my heart and now motivates my every day. I didn't expect it. I didn't ask for it. At times, I'm not sure what to do with it. But I do believe *She Did What She Could* is from God, and my commitment is to seek his leading in its expression and investment.

Others have been tenaciously at my side through the development of the concept, the writing, and the final expression of this book. There were many times when I couldn't seem to move ahead or didn't even know if I was supposed to. I am so grateful for their "picking up a corner of my mat" and taking me to Jesus as the paralytic's friends did for him in Mark 2.

To those who read and advised, thank you for your wise input. Kenna Barron, Valerie Bell, Dr. Craig Blomberg, Carla Foote, Carol Kuykendall, Karen Marchant, Evan Morgan, Naomi Cramer Overton, Kendall Parkhurst, Karen Parks, Shelly Radic, Dr. Liz Selzer, Georgia Skiles, Dr. Brian Stafford, and Philip Yancey, your investment made *She Did What She Could* tighter, clearer, more applicable to more people, and better biblically.

To Rick Christian and Lee Hough, thank you for representing *She Did What She Could* with such passion. And Lee, thank you for your valuable writing input in readying the first draft for the eyes of others.

To my friends at Tyndale—Carol Traver, Sue Taylor, Becky Nesbitt, Maria Eriksen, and Ron Beers—thank you for embracing *She Did What She Could* with your whole hearts. Wow!

And to the board, staff, field leaders, and volunteers of MOPS International, thank you for first receiving the message of *She Did What She Could*, then reproducing it in a movement of individuals whose lives were changed, and now wanting to make others different by SDWSC-ing every single day.

Introduction

SDWSC: Five Letters That Can
Change the World

Most of us care. We really do. We care about our own lives,
for sure, and also about the lives of those around us. We care
about poverty and injustice, about orphans and the sick. We
care about the folks who live and work alongside us and about
what happens in their families, in their hearts, and in their
heads. And yet, weighed down by everyday responsibilities—
bringing home a paycheck, putting food on the table, shuttling
kids around—we question our ability to make a difference.
When we're bombarded by the latest celebrity-help-the-world-
athon, we shrug our shoulders in futility. *Me? How?* Faced with
the seeming insignificance of what we have to offer, we don't
offer anything.

Maybe it's because we think that in order for it to count,
to make a difference that matters, we have to do something
big, or *everything* we could do, or something no one else
has done.

But that's not true.

The Backstory
What can we do?

I came to ask this question one night while watching the
NBC Nightly News anchored by Brian Williams. My kids were

off doing their own things elsewhere. My husband was traveling. I was sitting on my couch with a stack of files from work by my side and my dinner in front of me on the ottoman. It was a normal night of multitasking: eating dinner, working, and watching the news.

I heard Brian say something about a special report from Ann Curry of the *TODAY* show that was important enough to re-air in the evening. I looked up from my reading as Ann apologized for the pictures she was about to show—not exactly appropriate for the dinner hour. Then she launched into a tale of torture, describing the conditions of mentally retarded adults in Serbia, who were kept in cribs their *entire lives*. Across the screen came pictures of grown men in the fetal position, sucking their thumbs and rocking back and forth in frozen contortions.

"Some of these men have never been released from their beds," Ann commented.

How can this be? I found myself standing in the middle of my family room, hands raised in the air, *howling*. Then a sob erupted, and tears started down my face.

Now, I'm not a stranger to tragedy. I've sat at the bedsides of the elderly as they loosened their grip on their dignity—and on life. I've preached in rescue missions and prisons. I've traveled to Central America, South America, and the Caribbean and have witnessed firsthand the poverty and deep needs of the people there. Once I viewed the head of a horse, discarded by a butcher, in a muddy, rutted row of shacks. Another time I trudged through a jungle to visit a family consisting of three children, the oldest of which was seven years old. I gaped at the four-year-old cook stirring their dinner of beans while shooing flies off its surface. I've seen hard stuff before.

But something cracked me open that night, and like a foot jammed in a doorway, it wouldn't let me close back down.

Do something.

A week later I saw another story of human tragedy on CBS's *60 Minutes*: hundreds of thousands of Congolese women who were victims of multiple rapes.

How can this be?

And then I heard the head of the International Justice Mission, speaking about sex trafficking, say that twenty-seven million people have been sold into forced prostitution.

What?

During these unsettling weeks, as I heard of these soul-troubling tragedies, I had been working my way through a book in which one particular story demanded my return day after day. It wasn't a new tale. Actually, it was one I'd read many, many, *many* times. But in this particular season it somehow grabbed on to my soul, squeezing it tight and wringing from it a reaction that required attention.

The Story

She saw him across the room and immediately sensed a familiar awareness in the very core of her being. It wasn't romantic. It wasn't sexual. It wasn't "needy." It was more like a primal pull, a "knowing and being known" kind of drawing. From within her arose a conviction that here she faced a defining moment, an opportunity to somehow be better than she'd ever imagined she could be.

The room was thick with aromas from the meal, smoke from the grilled lamb rising in tendrils toward the ceiling. Conversation buzzed about her, punctuated by laughter and accompanied by background music.

Clutching the present she had prepared, she wound her way through the group that had gathered around him, approaching with confidence but not without concern. When she reached him, he looked up at her and smiled. The crowd shifted to make room for her but then drew in a collective breath as she presented the beautiful flask, a work of art in itself.

Without hesitation, she snapped the long neck off the vessel, and richly perfumed oil bubbled from the opening, dripping onto her hands. Then she raised the bottle and extravagantly tipped its contents fully on his hair. The fragrant potion oozed down his temples, his cheeks, and onto his neck. Lifting his gaze, he met her eyes and received her offering with gratitude.

A hollow silence, awkward and stiff, descended on the room. One from his inner circle of friends barked out an objection: "What a waste! Think how many hungry people could have been fed with what it cost!" His words gave permission to the other stunned observers so that murmurs of disapproval traveled through the room. Rejection and judgment rained down on her.

Again he met her eyes, understanding the meaning of her gesture better than anyone else present. "She has done a beautiful thing. Yes, her gift was expensive, but the money that went for it would never pay for the food needed for all the hungry in the world. She meant this as an offering uniquely for me, to prepare me for what I am facing. She did what she could. And because she did what she could, what she did will be remembered as long as I am remembered."

Everyone's Story

Jesus said that because "she did what she could," her action would be remembered as long as he was remembered. **S**he **D**id **W**hat **S**he **C**ould. **S-D-W-S-C.**

How many times had I read this story, heard it taught, or sat through a sermon about it and missed that sentence? I remembered the woman and her discomfort, her exposure. I remembered Jesus and his love for her. The perfume and its expense. The critical disciples and their judgmental comments. But this sentence—"She did what she could"—how had I missed it so many times?

As I read and reread it, I began to see Jesus' response to the woman in a way I hadn't before. He had defended the woman's action and pronounced that it would be paired with the Good News wherever it is preached throughout the world. It was so worthy, so accepted, so descriptive of God's love, that what she did would be permanently—eternally—attached to the Good News of God's gracious care for humanity.

Where else in Scripture is such a statement made? What was this beautiful thing that Jesus paired with the gospel? What did she do?

She did what she could.

Those five words hit me—hard. Rising up inside me and standing my heart at attention, they grabbed me and pushed me to a permanent paradigm shift.

She did what she could—SDWSC.

Whether it was related to the mentally retarded adults in Serbia, the ravaged Congolese women, the children enslaved by sex traffickers, the AIDS orphans, the starving millions, or any other seemingly unfixable need before me, I had caught a glimpse of a life-shaping concept in this story about a woman who did what she could.

I lifted the corner of this thought to discover a fuller, broader, more challenging, and yet more realistic question than I'd ever considered before. A question that promised an answer within my grasp, not beyond it.

What if?

She did what she could. What if I did what I could? And you did what you could? So that we did what we could? Not necessarily in the Congo or in Serbia, but right here, right now, wherever God has planted each of us—all of us?

What if?

PART 1

She Did What She Could

She did what she could.
  She was a girl.
  God chose a girl to act.
  God chose a girl to change the world.

1
She Did What She Could

God chose a girl.

Mary of Bethany. We know her from Scripture as the sister of hardworking, hospitable Martha, in Luke 10, and of "up from the grave" Lazarus in John 11. The setting is their home in Bethany, about one and a half miles from Jerusalem.

The event takes place just days before Jesus' Triumphal Entry into Jerusalem, where he was hailed as King, fanned with palm branches, and celebrated as Messiah, and a little more than a week before his death for the sins of all humankind:

> Jesus was in Bethany at the home of Simon, a man who had previously had leprosy. While he was eating, a woman came in with a beautiful alabaster jar of

expensive perfume made from essence of nard. She broke open the jar and poured the perfume over his head.

Some of those at the table were indignant. "Why waste such expensive perfume?" they asked. "It could have been sold for a year's wages and the money given to the poor!" So they scolded her harshly.

But Jesus replied, "Leave her alone. Why criticize her for doing such a good thing to me? You will always have the poor among you, and you can help them whenever you want to. But you will not always have me. She did what she could and has anointed my body for burial ahead of time. I tell you the truth, wherever the Good News is preached throughout the world, this woman's deed will be remembered and discussed." (Mark 14:3-9)

Though Simon could have been just another follower of Jesus, he is more likely the elderly—and healed—father of Mary, Martha, and Lazarus. According to John 12, the criticizing voice comes from Judas Iscariot, who, known to have been greedy and a thief, helped himself to what was in the disciples' money bag. Other references indicate that some of the disciples were critical of the extravagance of Mary's act.

Although the story is told from different perspectives and gives different details, depending on which Gospel account you read, one important detail remains the same: Here, at this juncture in human history, God chose a *girl* to pair with the preaching of the Good News for all time to come.

Do you realize what a *big* deal this is?

We expect God to use men. He has chosen men

historically and purposefully. Men to prophesy. Men to rule.
Men to lead. Men to follow a star across the wide world in
search of the Christ child. Men to fish for other men. Men to
form the church. Men to preach in the streets of early Christianity. The Bible is jam-packed with narratives and biographies and psalms of men, punctuated by an occasional female
rendition.

That's fine. It's good—no—it's *great*! Humankind has
much to learn from men. Men are *essential* to the expression
of God's image in our world and to his purpose for the planet.
And to be really clear—just because God chose a woman for
this particular story doesn't mean that he *didn't* choose men
to live out the message of this passage. As you read on in this
little book, you'll increasingly understand how the point of the
passage is that we—any of us—can change our world when
we finally "get" how much we are loved in a relationship with
God. God's love changes us. Radically. All of us. And when *we*
are different, we make a difference in our world.

But *oh* how refreshing it is to hear a story sung in
soprano! How healing and hopeful to see the curve of our own
reflection in the turn of a tale. How much easier to understand a message spoken in our "first language." Sans translation. Often, women have to interpret stories, teachings, and
illustrations from male to female—in church, in business, and
in life. Such "bilingualism" is part of our everyday lives. But
not here. Not this time. This story is first-person-female. The
main character is a girl. A heroine. A *she*.

God chose a girl. A woman. A sitter at Jesus' feet, in
contrast to a dissenter who betrayed him. And he paired her

with the telling of the gospel for all time to come. Jesus said, "I tell you the truth, wherever the Good News is preached throughout the world, this woman's deed will be remembered and discussed" (Mark 14:9). God chose a woman who acted on her love for him in response to his love for her.

If this grabs your attention today, just imagine how God's choice sat with the crowd just after the crossroads of time between BC and AD, when women were little more than property. Slaves. Chattel. In fact, tradition held that each morning, Jewish males offered a blessing that thanked God for not making them Gentiles, slaves, or women.

The fact that Jesus invited women to accompany him on his journeys around Israel was shocking in itself. But to actually receive his livelihood off their generosity, to include them in his teaching, to equip them to serve and share in his post-Resurrection Kingdom work—that was *radical*. That he paired a girl and her gesture of love with the telling of the gospel for all time forward—such a choice slid beyond the comprehension of those present then—or even of many people now, for that matter.

But *God chose a girl*. Mary. We know her from passages contained in several of the Gospels. The apostle John seemed closest to her, as he included her most often in his chronicles of Christ. She chose to sit at Jesus' feet and learn from him rather than scurry about preparing food for him and others, as did her sister, Martha. Of course, there's nothing wrong with cooking. It's just that Mary innately desired the connection of communication, of learning, of presence.

In receiving the relationship Jesus offered her, she

discovered access to a faith-filled kind of living, one that tee-tered between blind hope in some moments and tangible returns on her trust in others. She saw her brother, Lazarus, become ill, and she wailed for Jesus to journey to him and heal him. She knew he could. When he did not, she stood, wait-ing to learn from him yet again. Having already seen Lazarus's lifeless body sealed in a tomb, she watched Jesus weep at the loss of her kin—his friend—and absorbed in her soul how very much he truly cared. And then, stunningly, unexpect-edly, beyond her comprehension, she witnessed the miracle of Lazarus alive before her, clearly breathing, although his grave clothes were still intact. She would likely remember this moment later, on a bright morning at sunrise, outside another tomb.

God chose a girl. He had certainly called women for-ward to his Kingdom purposes before. Through Eve, life was born into the world. In Deborah, justice reigned over Israel. Through Bathsheba, a great king was brought forth. Rahab served to save God's people, as did Esther. Mary birthed God's son. Tabitha (Dorcas) and Priscilla carried forward efforts in the early church. And Mary, this Mary of Bethany, was paired with the gospel forever.

God chose a girl. A woman. Like me. Like you. Like your coworker or your subordinate or your boss. Like your neighbor or your child's best friend. Like your mother or your sister or your daughter or your aunt or your niece or your granddaugh-ter. God chose a girl to pair with the gospel forever. Look over your shoulder at her. Look in the mirror at her. Elevate her voice, her heart, her actions to the Kingdom possibilities they contain.

God chose a girl—and *she* did what she could.

● ● ●

She'd adopted him as a baby. Dimpled, chunky, and beautiful, he thrilled at the sound of her voice, her smell. He'd been a challenge to raise. Bright, creative, unendingly energetic, he delighted in the smallest life moments: discovering a caterpillar humping along a sidewalk on a summer afternoon, careering his plastic Big Wheel down the driveway, swinging higher and higher and higher at the park.

As he grew into his tween and then teen years, his talent for sports emerged: a stunningly fast fifty-yard-dash time. He made friends easily but had not been able to keep them without her help. Schoolwork demanded an attention and focus he didn't possess without the help of medication. He finished high school, finally, and flitted from this to that, from waiting tables to construction to trade school, all the while roller-coasting his moods with drugs and alcohol.

He was arrested for drunk driving and released without much penalty. Again. And again. He did jail time.

She knew he was still drinking. And driving. A danger to himself and to those around him.

From across the country, she called the Virginia Highway Patrol and reported his license plate and his habit. They noted her concern in their state's database, leaving her completely unsure whether or not her "mother's plea" had made any difference.

But she did what she could.

She **did** what she could.
    She acted.
    She didn't just think about acting.
    She didn't act out of obligation.
    She didn't let others act for her.
    She didn't wait to be invited.

2
She *Did* What She Could

Mary didn't just think about doing something. She didn't pledge to herself, *I'll do something sometime,* feel better in that moment, and then forget about it.

She didn't "take her turn" out of obligation. Or because she had to. Because it was the festival season and doing nice things was expected, even required.

She didn't vicariously invest through the gestures of others. Observing from a safe distance as other people invested would have been much easier. Less obvious. More expected. Far less risky.

She didn't wait to be invited. If she had, there would have been little question of the appropriateness of her action. Then the response of others in the room wouldn't have been her fault.

But if she thought and didn't act, she would regret not

offering the comfort she longed to give. If she had taken her turn out of obligation, the action would have lacked meaning. If she had stood as an observer rather than engage as a participant, she would not have experienced the personal satisfaction of involvement. If she had waited to be invited, she might never have moved, for she might not have been invited in the *expected* sense of the word.

Pushing past the paralysis that might have kept her body still, moving despite the objections in her head and the hesitations in her heart, she acted.

There was a *nowness* to her action. Recognizing that she was living in a moment that might never be repeated, she acted. Right then. When it would matter most to Jesus, she ministered to his body *before* his death. She seized the moment, knowing it was hers to invest.

What courage! What tenacity! Yes. There was that. For a woman to act with such abandon was truly bold in those days.

There was also a *naturalness* to her action. The verb tense used in the original language is one that describes a real event that actually transpired. This was an everyday action. Mary simply put her passion into play and did what she could.

She acted out of her love. She knew that Jesus loved her, and she loved him back. She *lived* loved. That's the whole point of the gospel, isn't it? Jesus' death on the cross giving humankind access to the one perfect God, who cannot tolerate imperfection or even unintended failure. The gospel is grace given to all in need of it so that they can—finally—return love to the Creator. Their Creator.

She *did* what she could. A verb. An action. Moving and implementing her love in a way that mattered, she *did*.

* * *

It had been a busy morning, even more so than usual. She'd dropped the boys at day care, her eldest now in a "hanging back" stage so that she'd nearly had to pry him off her leg as she left. As she headed to the office, she realized she was hungry and pulled into the drive-through. She merged quickly in front of another car, lowered her window, and ordered a breakfast burrito and a large Coke. Then, as she pulled forward, it hit her: She hadn't just *merged* in front of the sedan behind her; she had cut in front of it.

Oh my gosh! No wonder the other driver had glared at her— and gestured not too nicely. Even though she'd had a trying morning, she felt rotten. Sure, she might not ever see this person again, but it didn't seem right to just ignore her blunder.

Then the solution registered. She handed a five-dollar bill through her window and instructed the attendant to put the money toward the order of the driver behind her. There. Better. She pulled forward and watched in her rearview mirror as the driver leaned toward the window with an astonished expression and then turned forward with a smile.

Yes, better indeed. She did what she could.

She did **what** she could.
    She acted out of what she had, not
        what she wished she had.
    She did what she could, not all she
        could.

3
She Did **What** She Could

The "what" Mary chose is significant.

In parallel tellings of the story, her siblings chose their roles in the room. Her sister, Martha, served—a role familiar but reframed after Jesus' first visit to their home, when she had lost herself in the preparations and had missed out on Jesus' presence. Their resurrected and restored brother, Lazarus, reclined at the table, a symbolic centerpiece of what lay ahead for Jesus. Mary could again sit attentively at Jesus' feet—in the past, Jesus had praised her for choosing the "one thing worth being concerned about" (Luke 10:42)—or she could choose another role.

The "what" she chose shaped her role.

Picture her considering her options. She mentally sorts through her various skills: Could she dance or sing or recite something from the Hebrew Scriptures? Her thoughts pivot to her possessions, few truly valuable ones among them: her brush or her robe or a pot she had formed?

So not enough. None of it appropriate. If only she had more to choose from . . . something unique, expensive, worthy. She closed down her thoughts against the rationalization of what she didn't have and surveyed—honestly and carefully— what she did have. Then, from all the "whats" she possessed, she chose one specific "what" for the moment.

The flask of nard. *Yes*, she thought.

Nard was made from the aromatic oil extracted from the root of a nard plant, likely grown in India. A rose-red substance known as spikenard, it would have been the Chanel No. 5 of its day. Its going rate was three hundred denarii, which was equivalent to about a year's salary. Such a valuable essence was transported in a decorative flask or a box that was, in itself, a valuable work of art. Sometimes shaped like a flower or a rosebud, the alabaster or marble flask had a long neck and was actually sealed in such a way that the neck of the bottle had to be broken in order to access the perfume. Once it had been broken, there was no way to close it again— no cork, no lid, no stopper. Whatever wasn't used in the first application ended up wasted.[1]

A smile grew in Mary's heart as she settled on this particular gift to express her love for Jesus. It was a lavish gift. One that she herself likely had received from the hand of another and had saved, treasured, even, not wanting to open and enjoy it, since in doing so she would also spend the comfort of its promise.

She settled on her "what" and gave it without looking

back. There were no regrets. No *buts*. Just giving. Not from what she didn't have but from the one thing she had that would truly make a difference, speak her love, meet the need, compassionately connect to Jesus as he was facing what would no doubt be the most challenging moment of his life on earth.

Oh, and lest we send ourselves over the edge of self-sacrifice here, note that she did *what* she could. Not *all* she could.

Rather than give this—and that—and then some more, only to eventually fall, spent, at his feet, she gave what she could and left it at that. Enough. A lot. Just right. She chose *what* she could—and gave it ungrudgingly.

● ● ●

He noticed the cars lining the street, many more than normal. They streamed out of one driveway: his neighbors', two doors down. The one with the live-in elderly grandfather.

He must have passed away, he thought.

He sat on the bench on his porch, facing the house, and watched as folks flapped out the screen door and made their way to their cars, sputtered the engines, and drove up the street. A woman arrived in a minivan, hobbled around to the sliding door to withdraw a casserole, and then trudged up the steps. Children tumbled about on the lawn. A delivery person brought a flower arrangement.

He thought through his options. Not much of a cook, he had no food to prepare. Uncomfortable with caring for children, he turned away and stared thoughtfully into the air before him.

Then he rose and ducked into his own front door, made his way to his bedroom closet, and pulled down a wooden box from the top shelf. Tucking it under his arm, he headed back out, down his steps, and across the patchy grass between his home and his neighbors'. Up the steps, to the screen door. He looked inside at the small crowd chatting amiably, and met the eyes of the old man's daughter.

"I came to shine the shoes," he said.

"Shoes?" she asked with raised eyebrows.

"Yes, shoes. For the service. It's what I can do."

The woman smiled and opened the door wide, allowing him—with his wooden box of polish and brushes—to enter.

Following her to the kitchen, he waited while she made a quick trip through the house. Then, he settled down to shine the shoes. He did what he could.

*She did what **she** could.*
She was a specific woman with a
specific story who acted out of the
particulars of her life.
She acted because she knew she was
loved and wanted to love back.

4
She Did What *She* Could

Before we go any further, let's be clear about who "she" was. It's easy to get confused here. Because this story is told in three of the four gospels—Matthew (26:6-13), Mark (14:3-9), and John (12:1-8)—we sometimes assume that a similar story told in Luke 7:36-50 is the same story. But it's not. It's not the same people or the same setting, it didn't take place at the same time, and it doesn't have the same message. That's a shadow story about another woman who anointed Jesus.

Let's dive a little deeper.

Both stories take place in the home of a man named Simon. But our story occurs in the home of Simon the Leper (likely the once infirm and now healed father of Mary, Martha, and Lazarus), and Luke's story is about Simon the Pharisee.

In both stories, the central character is a woman. But

our story's heroine is Mary of Bethany, a good friend and follower of Jesus who knew him so well that she understood his impending death and the significance of her gesture of pre-burial anointing. Luke's story is of an "immoral," (some translations say "sinful") woman. We're never told her name. And though we're all "sinful," the underlying meaning of Luke's description refers to her reputation in the town—likely for prostitution. Mary of Bethany was not a prostitute. The sinful woman was not Mary Magdalene, either. Mary Magdalene was a woman from whom Jesus had cast out demons and who then became a follower (Luke 8:2).

Both stories depict a woman anointing Jesus with expensive perfume. We don't know where Mary of Bethany might have received the nard, but a prostitute could easily have been paid in perfume for her services and thus had it handy to bring forward to Jesus in the story in Luke.

Both stories describe the woman pouring the perfume on Jesus—sometimes on his head, sometimes on his feet. Anointing a guest with oil was customary in that culture, though usually with just a few drops on the head. In two of the three Gospels (Matthew and Mark), Mary of Bethany anoints Jesus' head. In John's Gospel, she pours the oil on his feet. Scholars suggest that this head-to-toe gesture made sense as people reclined at the table while dining in New Testament times. It also symbolized Mary's preparing Jesus' body for burial.

In Luke, the "sinful" woman washed Jesus' feet—a task usually performed by a slave or servant at the host's direction. In Jesus' remarks about the woman's gesture, he points out that he'd been denied this normal practice of hospitality prior to her effort. When she dried his feet with her loosened hair, the crowd was aghast, because a woman's unbound hair evidenced her loose-woman status and was socially inappropriate. Way too intimate for such a public gathering, perhaps the equivalent of greeting a stranger with a French kiss. But the woman's action resulted from her gratitude for Jesus' touch on her heart, a motivation he understood and received as she intended. (In a way, *this* woman also did what she could. . . .) In John's gospel, Mary of Bethany also wiped Jesus' feet with her loosened hair, but not because it was her habit to be provocative. Rather, she did so out of her relationship of spiritual intimacy.

So there we are: four Gospels, two Simons, two women, two jars of perfume, one Mary, one Jesus—and two separate stories.

Now let's get back to ours.

Mary of Bethany did what *she* could. She gave from the context of who God had made her to be—and from what her relationship with him was making her. She sat at Jesus' feet, opening her soul to his teaching, his wisdom, and his love. Because she took the time to take him in, she "got" him. Over the days and months and, perhaps, years of their relationship, his investment combined with the core of her being to yield a rich essence of character, from which she later anointed him in a moment of his own great need. Spiritual intimacy had been formed and in return, it formed her.

Because she had received love, she gave it. She understood what, so far, the disciples had missed. In this act of worship, she *lived* loved.

Mary approached Jesus with her gift of perfume and poured it out with confidence, her gesture expressing her love for him and preparing his body for burial before his death, the broken flask foreshadowing the shards customarily left in the tomb after the body's anointing for burial.[1]

Her gift touched Jesus in the moment, the fragrant oil running off his hair, down his temples and onto his neck and his chest, comforting him with love when it mattered most to him.

I wonder whether later, Mary's gift gave again: as Jesus prayed in a midnight garden setting, tortured by thoughts of what lay ahead and privately battling with his destiny. As he stood before the high priest, and then Pilate, then Herod, and then back before Pilate, enduring their ridicule and accusations. As the thorny crown was smashed down on his head. As he bent his back under the lashes of the whips. As he struggled to carry a heavy cross through the streets of Jerusalem and up a dusty hill. As he was laid out on that cross and fixed to it by heavy iron nails through his hands and feet. And as he hung in crucifixion.

As his head fell to his chest, dipping under the weight of his suffering, did any fragrance still linger, mingling with the stench of blood, and bring back, however briefly, that tender moment? In those hours of torture, when the soldiers taunted him by shaking wine before his parched lips, did the remembrance of her gift revive his soul? As he turned to the right and the left, taking in the two suffering with him and offering to each of them the hope of heaven, did any remaining fragrance convince his frail humanity of the truth of his own promise? As he looked down and beseeched his dear friend and follower John to take in his mother as his own and to care for her after his death, did any small part of the smell rise from his chest to his nostrils and warm him with comfort that, indeed, she would be held close in her grief?

Jesus gave Mary of Bethany access to himself. Because she had fully received all he'd held out to her in his presence and his teaching and his very being, she had been forever changed. She acted from the reality of the relationship she shared with him.

To Jesus, Mary gave a gift that kept on giving. She did what *she* could. She let him love her.

* * *

She slid into the booth, set her purse beside her, and took up the menu. It had been a good morning. Her idea had found favor with her boss. Likely there was a bit of a bonus in the works.

Within a few minutes she was joined by her lunch date. As they exchanged greetings, the waitress approached, slapped down two waters and then paused, jutting out a hip and requesting their drink order.

Something about their server drew her attention. Her hair stuck out in spikes from some kind of amassment atop her head, its brassy-blonde color contrasting to her salon-tanned skin. Thick eyeliner. Long fake nails. A smoker's voice. Hollow, pain-filled eyes.

After giving her drink and food order, she fell into familiar conversation with her friend, and the time passed quickly until the waitress returned to present the check. Plopping it down, she heeled and walked away, revealing a tear in her skirt and, further down, a hole in her black, gum-soled shoe.

After splitting the check with her friend, she scanned down the receipt to *Gratuity*, poised her pen, paused, poised it again, paused again, and then wrote in an amount equal to the check's total. She signed her name, flipped the folder shut, and sat back, oddly surprised but peaceful. No, she couldn't pay that much for a meal *every* day. After all, that bonus might never come. But today, she could. So, she did what *she* could.

She did what she **could**.
   She acted with what she had.
   She acted where she was.
   She acted when it mattered.

5
She Did What She **Could**

Mary grabbed hold of what she possessed—what was within her reach, under her power, obedient to her control—and she invested it. She did what she could with what she had to work with. She took the bottle of nard and made the most of it, right then and there.

Now, surely, she had other options from which to choose. Less valuable, less—well—less *extravagant*. This gesture was a little like wearing sequins to a picnic or pulling out the Dom Pérignon for a potluck. Mary gave to Jesus what was likely her most valuable asset—her pension. Her insurance. Her equity. Her savings. She gave up her goods to give Jesus what she could in a moment of significance and meaning unlike any other in his life or in hers. *Wow*. She could have *way* overdone here.

But as we've already stated, while the nard was expensive

and extravagant, it was *specifically* the right gift for this pre-death moment. When we look at the other elements in Mary's "could," her follow-through makes even more sense.

She acted with what she had—*where she was*. For Mary, this meant acting in public. Perhaps the thought had occurred to her in private as she prepared for the dinner, applying a dab of her "everyday" perfume to her neck. But it had then moved with her out into the group gathered for the meal, out into the open for all to see—and evaluate.

She could have played it safe, holding the gift until a more private moment, a less risky spot, free from scrutiny. But, no, she pulled out all the stops and plunged ahead into an act that would forever commit her to Christ as her motivation for living. Symbolically baptizing her soul before a room of observers, she gave testimony of her changed life. Marrying her heart to him, she vowed her loyalty, faithfulness, and commitment.

She acted with what she had: She acted where she was, and she acted when it mattered. She acted purposefully.

Was it a calculated moment? Had she preplanned the "sermon" she was about to offer? Probably not. In fact, a sermon of any kind was a very unlikely offering for her, the seemingly quiet sort. Yet her expression of commitment to Christ invited others to decide what they would do with him. Her action forced the hands of all present, moving them to either relationship or rejection. Who did they think Jesus was? Did they grasp what was at stake? Would they believe? Would they follow? Would they let him love them?

Judas led the rejection, accusing Mary of frivolous waste

during a Passover celebration at which, traditionally, gifts were given to the poor, not to each other. He had a point. Mary could have sold the perfume at a huge profit—enough to live on for a year—and then she could have given that entire amount to the poor. In fact, during this celebration season, such an action would have been valued and deemed highly appropriate. Righteous, even.

Yes, she could have loved Jesus by serving the poor. But she knew there would be other opportunities for that. In this week, on this night, the most compelling expression of her love for Jesus was to act in response to his love for her: To lavishly love him back in a tangible, lingering endowment would mean the most in this precise moment and then would help carry him through his suffering for her and for all humankind.

She recognized the juncture before her, chose her path of devotion to Jesus, and by her gesture, invited others to follow. An evangelist for living loved, she gave an "altar call" for all present to do the same—to demonstrate their commitment to being Christ followers by doing what they could. Her deed became paired with the gospel because it spelled out *how* to follow in everyday action.

She acted with what she had. She acted where she was. She acted when it mattered.

She did what she *could*.

* * *

She had served as a leader in the nonprofit effort for more than three years. Her heart had been twisted this way and that as she slugged her way through challenge after challenge, and her reward was the tangible growth of the staff she led. Of those involved in her ministry, 97 percent reported that they had grown in their faith. That was satisfying. *Deeply* satisfying.

But the troubled economy squeezed hard on the organization. Donations decreased to less than 60 percent of budget. Salaries were slashed. After months of trying every other option, she saw the dreaded words *reduction of workforce* on the memo handed down from the board of directors.

The memo contained a list with two headings: "Remaining Staff" and "Released Staff." She read the names on each, haunted as she saw her own suggestions appearing in one column or the other. As her eyes moved down the names of those to be laid off, she absorbed the reality of one name in particular and swallowed hard. *Shannon*. Hired only a few months ago, the newly married, pregnant young woman had recently been evicted and would need help to land on her feet after yet another setback.

She reached for her wallet, grateful that she'd been to the ATM the day before. But as she counted out the cash, she thought twice. It wasn't enough. She considered her own diminished salary and the needs of her own family. Then she reached for her checkbook.

She did what she could.

As a result of her action . . . she was
  ridiculed.
  As a result of her action . . . she was
  honored.

The relationship resulted in a response.

6
She Did What She Could

As a result of her action, she was . . . ridiculed.

Judas, Jesus' eventual betrayer, aims the first spear of criticism at Mary's gift. As if emboldened by his example, others join in, creating a clattering of verbal strikes fired at Mary's bent frame: *What a ridiculous waste! Completely unnecessary! So inappropriate! Outrageous! How embarrassing! Who does she think she is? She needs to get herself together! Someone do something! Stop it! Stop it now!*

Many socially minded sorts today might agree about the apparent waste of what would easily have provided a year's groceries for an average family. Moralists of our time might wince at the squandering of the lavish, designer-label offering when its value could have accomplished so much good. Reputable nonprofit organizations leverage such amounts every day for the maximum benefit. Any good financial manager could have come up with a smarter use for the funds.

Imagine Mary chewing her lip in concern as she reconsidered her gesture and the resulting ridicule.

But Jesus' response? "Leave her alone." A command. Instead of telling *her* to stop, he orders that *they* cease their abuse—their blaming, sighing, enraged criticizing—of her.

"Why criticize her for doing such a good thing to me?" he asks in Mark 14:6. Instead of wondering about her action, he questions their intrusion into a sacred moment of ministry. Their paining, troubling, wearying of her—and him—in contrast to her comforting of him. Their heads, full of picky, irrelevant debate, in contrast to her heart, full of love.

As for the "waste" of the perfume in a time when the poor could have benefited from the investment, Jesus compared the poor—who would always be around and whom they could help whenever they wanted—with his own temporary earthly presence. What is ever wasted when it is invested at the only possible time—today?

As a result of her action . . . she was honored.

Look into Judas's face the way Jesus might have seen it, and you wonder at his gall. He was willing to sell out the one he should have seen as his King for thirty silver coins—about 120 days' wages—whereas Mary blessed the Lord she loved with a gift worth closer to a year's salary. Judas, who as "treasurer" held the responsibility of stewarding the money for the movement, could have—maybe should have—initiated a customary outpouring to the underserved during this feast time. Who really loved the poor more?

Jesus pronounces Mary's action "a good thing." Literally, he defines it a "noble" thing. The perfect thing to do in the moment. Mary knew that she was loved, and she responded to God's embrace by loving him back—right then, when he needed it and could receive it. *She did what she could.*

Jesus pairs her action with the telling of the gospel from that time forth. On the surface, this seems an odd pairing: A girl, and the gospel? A lavish outpouring of oil, and salvation? In the umpteen times you may have heard the story of Jesus, of his life, death, and resurrection, how often have you heard Mary's gesture included?

Both Matthew and Mark include this pronouncement. Could they simply have meant every time *their* Gospels were proclaimed, her act would be included? Maybe. But what if they meant that *Jesus* was making this pairing? What might Jesus have meant? Perhaps he meant that every time the gospel—the Good News of present help and eternal hope through Jesus' death on the cross for our sins—is proclaimed, it will be paired with the radical reality of Mary's relationship with Jesus, the kind of relationship that we, too, can enjoy. Jesus paired the gospel with a relationship of love that expresses itself in loving service. Salvation is not fire insurance, a ticket to heaven, a transaction to eternal life. Salvation is being transformed by a relationship of love.

Jesus paired Mary's loving act with the gospel for all time because, plain and simple, the gospel is love lived out.

She did what she could when she could. And because she did, she was ridiculed—and honored. So, now what? Exactly. Now . . . what?

If she did what she could—when she could—what difference would it make if I did what I could? How might what I could do connect to the expression of hope and love available in Jesus for others to see, to grab hold of, to integrate into their beings and doings?

What if *I* did what I could?

PART 2

What If
I Did
What I
Could?

What if . . .
   I did what I could?
   I'm a girl.
   What would it mean for me to act?
   What if I could change the world?

7
What If . . .
I Did What I Could?

What if *I* acted? I'm a woman whom God loves. What if I just start there: I am loved.

I used to think such a thing was silly, immature, unnecessary. Unworthy me? Loved by God? Humph! Shame would gurgle up in my soul against such a thought. In seconds, a "shame fest" would overtake me, quietly and in secret, and I felt like a child caught in a naughty act.

Mary's action shifts me away from that shame. It's not that I deserve to be loved. I don't. She didn't. No one really does. It's just that Jesus loves me. It's a fact. When I realize that I'm not so darling in and of myself and that I don't have to be—but that I am still irrevocably loved and valued and created for good—in such moments his love becomes all the more stunning to me.

What if *I* did what I could?

Wait—me? I'm just a girl. Exactly. In Mary, God chose a girl. I like describing her this way. A girl. It seems so much more doable than saying God chose a *woman*. Somehow, I can't relate to that word. When I hear the word *woman*, suddenly the effort feels too big, too responsible, and too hard for me. Issues of what it means to be a grown-up *woman* weigh down my shoulders. The littleness in me squirms in discomfort at the idea of this pressurized role. Childhood worries and inadequacies whirl around me. I go all prepubescent. Before I can even inventory my offerings, when I hear *woman*—I'm done.

So I start with *girl*. I can *be* a girl. I *am* a girl. A female in the process of growing into the world of the word *woman*. I can be that.

God chose a girl. God chose me. To do what *I* could. So what could *I* do? Let me think: *I* am middle-aged. *I* am a wife. *I* am a mother. *I* am a grandmother. *I* run a nonprofit ministry organization. *I* can write and speak and make awesome mashed potatoes. *I* am the child of divorced parents and the product of a home riddled with alcohol abuse. *I* carry with me emotional bruises from intangible wounds, and *I* also have experienced great healing and power over these afflictions.

I am creative. An original kind of thinker. An effusive leader. A passionate strategist. An energetic visionary. There are some pretty good things there. But what about the other parts of me?

I am impatient, controlling, and judgmental at times. *I* can be insecure and disrespectful. *I* am selfish. Sometimes insincere, know-it-all-ish, and shortsighted.

Doing what *I* could means bringing me, all of me, to the realization that I am loved by God and that from that love, *I* can act. The good, fun parts of me and the not-so-great parts of me too.

What if *I* did what I could?

I grew up in Houston, Texas. My days started with the sound of my mother's alarm clock blaring from way down the hall in our ranch-style home. I pushed back my covers and padded into the kitchen, where I found a glass, filled it with ice cubes, and poured Coke to the top. I grabbed a couple of chocolate chip cookies and made my way back down the hall to my mother's room, where I set this "breakfast" on her night-stand, turned off the alarm, and began the process of trying to shake her awake.

I was ten or eleven years old. My mother and father had divorced when I was five. My mother had lost herself in alcohol, and it had become my job to get her up and off to work in the morning.

For years, I mothered my mother and yearned for the very occasional visit from my father. My mother tried to mother us. She created Christmas celebrations filled with magic and fun that blearily faded into the topaz glow of Scotch as Christmas Day culminated. She did what she could to offer us a home and a hope for our lives.

I was by no means a perfect daughter—but I was a good one. There were times when I did what I could for my mother: waking her up in the morning, watching over my younger brother when she was unpredictable, cooking dinner when she was unable to do so. There were other times when what

I could do really meant *not* doing something: not letting my mother's instability prohibit my choice to leave and begin my own life. Not being "nice" but rather allowing some distance to grow between us in order for me to find my way out of codependency. Not accepting whatever she gave but instead insisting on certain boundaries in how she handled herself in my home when she visited my children, her grandchildren.

I know that though I am scarred in some ways, my offerings have been formed out of the very "me-ness" of my upbringing. My mother's illness shaped my resilience. I am who I am, with my strengths and my deficits, because of her— both her strengths and her deficits.

While I'm "better," healed of much, I am still being shaped. All that hangs back as unworthy in me finds the hope of healing that comes in a relationship with Jesus. All of me is welcomed by all of him.

What if . . . from the reality of who I am and who I have become—all of it—*I did what I could*? The question is unsettling—prodding, annoying, challenging—and then, somehow, freeing.

And you? What would it mean for *you* to do what *you* could?

No, you're not all you want to be, nor are you some superstar. You're *you*—okay in some areas and not in others. You, with the polka-dot track record of efforts, some successful, others not so much. You, with the great intentions and the occasional follow-through. You, with the past. You, with the present. You, with the commitments that stretch into the future. What about you?

Think about David—with deep potholes of adultery and murder behind him—looking at the road ahead and wondering how God could use him. Peter—Mr. Denial in the moment when Jesus could have used a good word—reinstated to be the earthly head of the church. Rahab—used just as she was, prostitute status and all—to save the spies of Israel.

Or Mary. Just a girl whom God chose to pair with the gospel because she did what she could.

Or me. A once-upon-a-time-girl-now-middle-aged-woman whom God tapped to train, to marry, to mother, to lead, to speak, to write, to love, to listen, to learn.

● ● ●

Sometimes it's in everyday situations, when I'm taking out the trash and notice the neighbors' sprinkler is overflowing into the street. So I go knock on their door and tell them. Sometimes it's in heroic surprise as my feet run to the side of a swimming pool and I lunge into the water to pull a toddler back to the surface, all under the glazed-over gaze of a lifeguard who missed it. Sometimes in a stunning moment I realize *I'm* the one to apologize to my husband for making a rude comment, or leave work to rescue my sick grandson at daycare, or stand up and speak at a meeting.

Me.

What if *you and I* did what we could—because we are loved?

What if . . . I **did** what I could?
  What if I acted?
  What if I didn't just think about acting
    but actually acted?
  What if I didn't act out of obligation?
  What if I didn't let others act for me?
  What if I didn't wait to be invited?
  What if I didn't just wonder about
    what difference I could make but
    actually took a step?

8
What If . . .
I *Did* What I Could?

I'm standing in the shower and thinking of calling a couple that has been through a tough time with their kids. I know it would mean a lot to them. I don't have solutions to their problems, but I know from my own experience that the companionship of someone who has "been there" is still meaningful. I decide to invite them to come for dinner. I don't plan to pronounce a solution over their world; I know I can't. But we can listen, my husband and I.

As I lather my hair, I think through my schedule and mentally select a few dates to double-check. I even get as far as planning a menu. There. Good.

I exit the shower, dress, and leave for my day. I check off meetings and tasks and other items on my to-do list. I drive home. The evening passes. Another day. And another. And I don't call.

Why? No real reason. The whole matter leaves the front of my mind, and I kind of forget about it—until I run into the mom unexpectedly and I feel my face redden at the reminder of my inaction. Does she notice? I ratchet up the compassion in my face and ask some specific questions about her daughter to prove that I really have been engaged in what she's going through, even though I've done nothing to demonstrate my concern.

I decide too much time has passed to act now. It would be awkward. When the faces of these family members appear in my mind, I pray for them. I wonder how the whole thing is progressing—and still I don't act.

But what if I *did* what I could?

What if I didn't just think about it; what if I actually *acted*? I'm not talking about "fixing" her daughter or curing her son. I'm just talking about doing what I could. Fix a meal. Give her a hug. That would be something. It would likely be enough.

I have lots of great ideas that I never follow through on. But what if I did?

What if I didn't just do what I was obligated to do but actually invested and did something that I knew would matter? Like planning my day so that when I attend an event, I can stay for the whole thing rather than just dash in and out to make an appearance. Like hanging out at church before or after the service in order to connect with people who could use some friendship. Like listening for the real response beneath the "fine" I receive when I ask a coworker how he's doing.

What if I didn't take the easy road of allowing everyone else around me to invest? What if I didn't excuse my own lack of action with the rationalization that what I could have done and didn't was really unnecessary, repetitive, or unvalued anyway? *They have enough canned food. Nobody will notice if I don't volunteer in my child's class this year. My twenty-five dollars won't make a dent.*

What if instead of waiting to be invited, I jumped in, took the initiative, volunteered, offered my two widow's mites?

As I look back at my life, I can trace a pattern of requests preceding nearly all my involvements: Would you serve on the committee? Would you give your money? Would you help? A call. A question. An invitation. I tended to conclude that initiating action on my own was, well, pushy, bossy, even arrogant. Who did I think I was?

But Mary wasn't "invited." Strictly speaking, Jesus never said, "Hey, Mary, would you please do something especially outstanding for me right now? Something I can hold up as an example for all time to come?"

God gives all of us skills, talents, gifts, possessions, personalities. He creates us to be and to do, and to braid our being into our doing and our doing into our being. I don't wait to be invited to "be." Why would I have to wait to be invited to "do"?

A friend meets my eyes and offers a challenge: "What can you do that no one has ever invited you to do?" I make a list. I am amazed at the variety of very doable tasks I tally. I can put colors together in a room or an outfit. I can use word pictures to describe feelings and situations in ways that communicate clearly. I can see where efforts are headed before they get there. I can identify forces motivating relationships and negotiate through them. Most days, nobody specifically asks me to invest these abilities. Does that mean I shouldn't bring them forward?

Perhaps I need to grab hold of the reality that what God has *equipped* me to do, he has *invited* me to do.

What if I moved beyond all these obstacles—thinking about acting but not acting, acting out of obligation, figuring someone else will act so I don't need to, and waiting to be invited in order to act? What if I actually took a step? What if . . . I *did* what I could?

What gap would be filled? What need would be met? What answer would be offered? What question would be asked?

Just recently another friend prodded me to stay in a selection process for a position I felt was out of my league.

"Why?" I pushed back. "I'm not a good fit. It's silly."

"Because," she said, "your presence in the process will help reveal who the right candidate is."

Hmm. I'd never considered that.

And you. What if you *did* what you could? What if you didn't just think about acting but actually followed through?

In our minds, we make it so hard, don't we? We think we have to *plan it out*. We have to *try harder*. In reality, there are opportunities all day, every day, right in front of us. Opportunities to just do what we could. Or maybe even to stop doing something in order to create space to do what we could.

Not convinced yet? Okay. What if you *didn't* do what you could? *Ugh.* Here comes the guilt. There are so very many "she *didn't* do what she could" stories, in my life—and in yours. They point the finger of accusation at us, and we squirm in discomfort.

● ● ●

She had been visiting a friend in the hospital, and as she walked toward the elevator, she felt the heaviness of all that lay ahead: more chemo, more family juggling, fewer resources to meet the need. She punched the down arrow, lifted her head, and focused on a man in a wheelchair to her left. He must have been in his sixties—maybe seventies. Clearly he was in pain as he hunched in his chair, his gnarled fingers combing his matted hair back from his brow, his mouth a grimace, his eyes slits.

Forgetting for a moment her own burden, she sensed a pull to go to him, to put her hand on his shoulder and utter a simple prayer of peace and healing over his soul.

Then, as if shrugging inwardly, she dismissed the tug she had felt. She was a stranger to this man. He would think her odd. The elevator doors opened, and she stepped inside. Adjusting the familiar mantle of her friend's illness about her shoulders, she selected her floor.

But like a photograph framed on a wall in her mind, the image of that man haunted her. Two days later she could still see him as clearly as she had in that moment at the elevator. And two months later, a vague grief continued to pull at her heart. *Why hadn't she obeyed the instinct?*

＊ ＊ ＊

He was driving home from the office, in a hurry to make his daughter's homecoming dinner at the holidays. How he had missed her! Her first semester away at college had been planned with a measure of expectation that life at home would be different. But her launch out of the nest had torn a surprising hole in the fabric of his days.

The snow accumulating on his windshield made driving a challenge, but the road was familiar, and he felt a purposeful confidence moving him along. Then, through the snow, he saw something on the side of the road. In the twilight he made out a car—some no-brand, two-door model—with part of its body raised, like a dog hiking its leg. *Flat tire*.

He slowed to take in the details: two people, one clearly a young woman. And the other? Surely a man—yeah—that looked like a guy helping.

Speeding up again, he glanced in his rearview mirror and wondered. *Was* it a guy? It had been hard to tell in the swirling snow. Did they have a spare? Should he have stopped?

He thought about it all the way home. And later that night, after chili and coffee and catch-up conversation, he went to bed, still wondering if a girl like his daughter had made it to her destination after all, or if she'd been stranded in the snow.

Nobody's going to do life 100 percent perfectly all the time. There are plenty of moments when it makes good sense for us to punch the elevator button, descend to our cars, and go home after a grueling hospital visit. Plowing through a snowstorm to meet our newly returned, precious child is completely understandable. I don't think anyone expects you or me to do and do and do and do what can be done, just so we won't feel haunted or bugged or bad.

And it's not just regular folks like you and me who don't do what we can. The disciples didn't stay awake in the garden of Gethsemane with Jesus—as he'd asked them to. The Bible traces story after story of God's very messed-up people not doing what they could. Peter didn't admit he knew Jesus in the Temple square. John Mark didn't remain on Paul's second missionary journey but for some reason abandoned him. Moses didn't control his anger. David didn't resist his attraction to Bathsheba.

So welcome to the club. We all blow it. SDWSC is not about guilt avoidance. It's not about paying it forward or doing random acts of kindness or living a better life. It's not about obedience just for the sake of obedience.

If I *did* what I could, I would be acting out of God's love for me in a given moment when he has more for me to experience. More, because I move beyond considering to engaging. More, because I invest out of an attitude of caring rather than out of a sense of obligation. More, because I act instead of letting someone else act. More, because I initiate, knowing that because I *am*, I can *do*.

More, because I do instead of don't.

What if I *did* what I could?

What would it mean if I *did* what I could? What if you *did* too?

What if . . . I did **what** I could?

What if I quit focusing on what I don't have and considered instead what I do have?

What if I let go of the pressure to do everything I could and instead did the one thing I could do now?

What if I started right now, in this moment, in this season of life, to do what I could?

9
What If . . .
I Did **What** I Could?

What? What could I possibly do that would make a difference today? Twenty-four million people die of starvation every day. I don't have a fancy jar of oil worth a year of my wages. What *do* I have? What is my "nard"?

I have a house, a car, an income, my health. But I need those things. What can I do when I don't think I have anything I don't need? Does God expect me to give the most expensive thing I have? My best stuff—and only my best stuff?

Let's look at the flip side: I'm exhausted, broke, scared, busy. What can I give out of what I *don't* have? More time? More effort? More trying? I'm too tired to think about more of anything. I don't have any "more."

In John 6, the "what" for a young boy on a hillside was his lunch: five barley loaves and two fish. Five thousand men (not to mention the women and children present, who typically were not counted in New Testament times) had listened most of the day to Jesus speak of hope and freedom and truth and light. They listened through lunchtime and on into the dinner hour without taking time to refuel. When Jesus' followers pointed this out to him, he told them to feed the people, which to the disciples seemed a ridiculous directive—until Jesus multiplied that young boy's lunch into a veritable smorgasbord for the hungry crowds. The boy's "what" fed tens of thousands of hungry men, women, and children.

So, what's my "what"?

The element of faith comes into play here. My "what" may not look like much to me. It may seem puny. It may look like no big deal, as if it couldn't make a dent. But when I put my "what" in Jesus' hands, it becomes enough.

I've experienced this over and over in parenting. I'll be running on empty—with a capital *E*—and then along comes a child needing my "what." So I offer it, and most of the time, it's enough. I remember staring into my pantry one night, hoping for dinner inspiration for my "starving" five-year-old son. Plunking down a plate of Top Ramen and chunk pineapple in front of him, I sat next to him, and we bowed our heads for grace. He looked up at me and said, "You are the best cook in the world, Mom—no, you're the best *mom* in the world!" *Go figure*, I thought.

I actually think back on this put-my-what-in-Jesus'-hands principle a lot as a mom, even though my children are adults now. I don't have enough. I can't make a dent, so to speak. I can't pay off their debts. I can't find them jobs. I can't heal their wounds from painful relationships. But I *can* invest in their lives, with faith and trust that God will match my offering to the need before me.

What if I did what is before *me* today? What if I let go of the pressure to do *everything* I could and instead did the *one* thing I could do now? That helps. It takes the focus off of giving *everything* and places it on giving *the one thing* that would matter right now, in this moment. After all, on another occasion, Jesus commended Mary for choosing to do the "*one* thing worth being concerned about" when she sat and learned at his feet (Luke 10:42, emphasis added). I could keep my grandson for the evening to give my daughter and her husband a "free" date night. I could pick up a birthday balloon for a coworker. I could offer a sincere compliment to the person in line behind me. I could grab an extra burger so I'm not empty-handed at the traffic light where the homeless hang out. Those "whats" are not so big. Not so impossible. Not so crazy-beyond-my-capacity. But will they be enough?

Sometimes I think that if I don't give *everything*, I'm somehow cheating God. I'm compromising. I'm selling out. I'm lazy and corrupt and just basic "slime." It's stunning to realize how easy it is to do *nothing* because I self-incriminate about not doing *everything*!

In most circles, some 80 percent of the people do only 20 percent of the work, and the remaining 20 percent do 80 percent of the work. In whichever slot we fall—"underly overinvolved" or "overly underinvolved"—we focus either on *nothing* or on *everything* and miss seeing our "what," the slot that lies between nothing and everything, where we live out our lives most of the time.

It also helps to remember that most of the time we don't know the importance of our "what" until after we do it. And sometimes not until *way* after we do it. A coworker stopped me in the hall to tell me that one day a few months ago, when I had simply stopped to ask about her and then had actually listened to her response, she'd been really close to quitting. I'm ever so glad now that I did that, even though I had no idea how much it was needed at the time.

What's my "what"? Maybe it depends on the moment and on what is needed in that moment. What if I give connection and empathy to someone who needs to feel heard and understood? At times that's really "expensive" for me. Most of the time, I have no space in my life to listen. But I listen anyway. And that makes a difference.

● ● ●

Becky struggled to identify her "what" between lots of would-be "whats."

First it was a Friday-afternoon request in the hallway at school while she was picking up her second grader: "Can you bring a batch of cookies next Monday for the teachers?" She agreed and headed her child to the van to make the next stop.

Then it was a phone call from someone asking her to help out in the nursery on Sunday. It seemed the flu was going around, and the department head sounded desperate. Okay.

As they were pulling in the driveway, her preteen remembered a homework project that required poster board, so Becky put the car in reverse, backed out of the driveway, and headed to the store.

Later, when her husband fell asleep on the couch during the game and Becky saw his tired face, she went ahead and mowed the lawn, even though it was "his" job.

Dinnertime came and went. Dishes were done, and the laundry waited. But when she answered the phone, she heard her panicked neighbor's voice pleading with her to come babysit while they raced to the emergency room with one of their children, who'd apparently had some kind of seizure.

Leaving the piles of laundry, Becky did what she could. She hurried next door.

Which "what" was Becky's "what"? How do you know?

When I asked about her "what," she said that it wasn't until the very end of that Sunday night, when she'd reviewed a litany of "whats," that she realized it was this last one that had truly been the bull's-eye on her "what" target: The call from her neighbor, arising from their relationship, communicated a need that Becky alone could meet.

What is your "what"? My "what" may be different from your "what." And yours may not be the same all the time.

● ● ●

One night, after Bible Study, Kendall desperately needed to breast-feed her baby. But her friend was hurting, and Kendall was the only one her friend would open up to. Could Kendall sit with her in her car and listen, and then pray with her? Yes, she could. She grabbed the baby and the diaper bag, headed for the car, and did *what* she could.

● ● ●

Alexandra normally spent five dollars a week on a specialty coffee. It was her Friday-morning splurge. But one day she wondered, *What if I wrote a check for more than I normally give to a cause and then cut back on something for "me" to underwrite the extra amount?* After some consideration, she decided to take the money she would have spent on coffee and give it to MOPS (Mothers of Preschoolers), International. That's $20 a month, approximately $240 a year. Alexandra did *what* she could. And it added up.

● ● ●

Lisa asked herself, *What if I went through my closet and culled things I haven't worn for at least a year? Then, instead of just dropping them off at the thrift store, what if I thought of people who wear my size and really need those items and gave the clothes to them?* That's *what* she did.

My presence. My coffee money. My clothes. My "what" can change from day to day, even from minute to minute. I can discover my "what" when I attend to what is happening around me and to what is in my possession that can make a difference at a particular moment. What if I did *what* I could?

What if . . . I did what **I** could?

What if I offered my story and my skills?

What if I didn't wait until I had it right or finished or perfect?

What if I believed God loved me so much that I wanted to love him back by doing what I could?

10
What If . . .
I Did What *I* Could?

I'm a woman, created by God, shaped by life, and equipped by all I've experienced. What if I invested *me*—who God has made me to be and how my relationship with Jesus is making me today—in what I am facing?

It was 1989. I remember that my hand was on the phone and I was preparing to make a call. I was more than a bit nervous. I had been hosting a radio program for a local grad school, and the decision had been made to drop it for budgetary reasons. But with about five years of programming already "in the can," I thought it would be silly to just let it go, and I very much wanted to see the program adopted by another institution. I also needed the money.

So with my hand on the phone, I prayed that God would make a way for the program to continue. It would take some major miracle work on God's part. I was a nobody. Who would want that program?

Just as I was ready to punch in the number, the phone rang. I jumped—answered it, and discovered that the caller was a board member of MOPS International (a lifestyle evangelism and leadership-development ministry for moms of preschool age children), inquiring about my interest in the position they had open for president—of the whole shebang. The person chosen would be the first president of the grassroots effort that had begun some fifteen years earlier.

Me? Ha! Me? The daughter of an alcoholic mother? Me? The mother of two young adopted children (three and five), who wasn't quite sure how well she was doing in that new role? Me? Lead an international mothering organization?

It sounded preposterous! But because of how the call had come, in the exact moment when I found myself at a juncture between one job and the next, I responded that I would pray about it and that I would be open to considering it.

I began to look—really look—at the mothers around me. In the grocery store one afternoon, with my own children leaning out of the cart to try to reach the temptations in the checkout line, I examined the other moms, in sweats, in jeans, in professional attire, juggling this and that and more, and all the while mothering their hearts out.

I felt God was saying to me, "Look at them. They have the same Swiss-cheese holes in their souls that you have in yours. Give to them out of all of you, out of what you know and what you don't know. Let even your deficits be your offering."

What if I did what *I* could? The question forced a response then. It still does today.

I, a daughter of divorce and alcoholism. The sister of multiple whole, half-, and stepsiblings. The wife of a man whose great love for me leaves me humbled. The mother of two children I didn't carry but could never lay down. A leader formed as much by codependent meanderings as by good, pure efforts.

What if I offered *my* unique offering, beginning right here and right now—honestly, unapologetically, and freely— because *I know that I know that I know* that I am loved, so much that I choose to live loved?

I served as president and CEO of MOPS International for twenty years. During my tenure, I invested my ability to speak persuasively in order to communicate the vision for the mission to others. I asked for and received loyalty from the staff and from the enormous wave of hundreds of thousands of moms, because I knew such a following was necessary for accomplishing the mission.

I made mistakes, lots of them. I plunged ahead when I should have waited. I was shortsighted because I thought I had the whole picture and I didn't. But in both my good moments and my not-so-good ones, in flush seasons and frugal ones, I gave *me* to the ministry and watched God make *me* enough.

King David started out as a shepherd. As a boy, he protected his sheep from danger. In the lonely days and nights in the meadows, he leaned into his own Shepherd and received protection and provision. He drove lions and bears away from the flock, rescued lambs from their mouths, and fought and killed the predators with a club (see 1 Samuel 17:34-36). Anointed as king when he was just a teenager, he drew from this early experience as a shepherd when it came to protecting his people: He picked up five stones, hurled one from his sling, and knocked a giant out cold. He did what he could.

Later in his life, resting on his earlier accomplishments, he foolishly gave in to his own passions with Bathsheba, committing first adultery and then murder. Yet from such a season of blunder, God later brought forth David's successor, Solomon, who became known as the wisest king of Israel, responsible for beginning the collection of our "proverbial" wisdom.

When we live loved, we splash in the puddle of our personhood, and smeared with the stains of our humanity, we rise to find God forming all of what we are into an offering that somehow shapes the world around us for good.

What would it mean for you to do what *you* could? You, the child of _____, or the sibling of _____, or the spouse of _____, or the parent of _____, or the grandparent of _____. What do you bring to this world in the offering of *you*? How has God redeemed who *you* are in such a way that it can be invested, all of it, for his purposes? How does he want to meet you in the messiness of who *you* are in order to shape your unique investment?

If you're not sure, put the book down for a minute, and really think about what *you* can offer. . . .

Are you back? I can hear your objections now: Oh no, you say. You don't know what I've done—the choices, the messes, the secrets. Why, just yesterday—*no way*. It's too messy. I don't want to get involved. I might get hurt, and I'm *done* with getting hurt.

Forget it, you decide. You'd rather go it alone— uninvolved, controlling the flow of life and love and therefore the ramifications for your soul.

I know. In the months that preceded our move into our current home, I had a dream. Or maybe I should say I encountered the first episode of what would become a recurring dream. Our children were teens, busy with school and friends and all that went with them. Our home was under construction, and more than once I had walked through the framed-out floor plan of our new home, imagining what would go where. Life was chaotic. It's no wonder even my sleep was filled with dreams about planning and preparing.

One night, a dream took me on a tour up the wooden stairs to the newly erected walls that formed the bedrooms. In my dream, God said to me, "These rooms are for your daughter and her baby."

"She isn't pregnant!" I answered.

"Yes, she is," came the reply.

When I awoke, I shook off the dream, dismissing it as a consequence of too much stress, and went about my day as usual.

Another night not long after, I dreamed again. This time I was walking with God in the basement of the unfinished house. Again I heard him say, "These rooms are for your daughter and her baby."

"No, she's not pregnant," I replied, but when I awoke, I wondered. . . .

Later that day, when my daughter approached me saying that she felt "funny," I drew a deep breath and asked her if she could be pregnant. To my stunned surprise, she nodded. Hours later I sat with her in the doctor's office as the results of a test registered—and so did the reality.

Like most moms who think their kids would never go in such a direction, I flipped out. It didn't help that I was heading up a mothering organization. I didn't want my daughter to be pregnant. I didn't want to be a grandmother. I didn't want my teenage son, a few years younger than my daughter, to suddenly become an uncle. No.

I didn't feel loved, nor did I want to live loved. I wanted to hide my daughter, my family, and me. I didn't want to lead a mothering organization, involving zillions of moms just setting out on the journey of motherhood, while making my way through what I defined as "ruin."

My daughter had her baby, and she and her son lived upstairs for the first two and a half years of his life—in the very rooms that it seemed God had set apart for them. My husband and I parented our daughter and grandparented our grandson, and when they eventually moved out on their own, we continued to do so over the two-mile distance that stretched between us. Later, she married, and they became a family—my grandson, my daughter, and her new husband.

Gradually—make sure you note that word *gradually*—I realized that I'd been given a relationship with yet one more mother of preschool-age children, that she'd been "born" right under my own roof, and that her presence in my days would provide a deeper understanding of the audience I served.

But this experience wasn't just about other people. It was also about me. Just as space had been created in our new home for my enlarged family, space was also being created in *me*. Over time, I began to understand how even in this unexpected "expectancy," there was so much *good*. So much *more*. So much *love* to live out.

I now had even more *me* to offer. What if I did what *I* could?

We sometimes forget that doing what *we* could means living loved. It's not always easy, or even comfortable. But when our action arises out of a relationship of love, stunning possibilities emerge. Fear fades into the background. Options grow. Choices flow. Suddenly we know—and so we go.

Layer after layer, love builds our lives, and our lives build our love. Today we have more to offer than we did last week or last year or a decade ago.

When I came into marriage, I had a rather meager version of love to share: romantic, in the moment, restricted by my own limits. Thirty years later I am fuller, freer, more forgiving. I forget to keep score—finally. I am now able to move beyond annoyance over my husband's quirks, understanding that they are just part of him and who he is rather than elements in some grand scheme of selfishness, out to take me over and win.

In my leadership, I move less definitively and work to allow greater room for the contributions of others. I pause to listen more. I ask questions and leave blank spaces.

My mothering is now more like "familying." Rather than try to maintain the tightly knit foursome of our early years, when I sweated every stitch of my efforts and tied us together with a furious commitment, today I am able to relax in the assurance that who we are has already been woven. We can stretch more than we could ever imagine. The comings— planned and unplanned—won't ruin the structure. The goings won't tear us apart beyond the healing power of love.

Try combing through the various layers of *you*. (It's not necessary to pull out your Myers-Briggs Type Indicator or do an online inventory of your skill set. Just take a look at *you* and what *you* can offer.) What if *you* did what only *you* could do? What would happen that could have happened no other way? What could occur through *you*? What might develop in *you* if *you* did what *you* could?

We so often count ourselves short. We tend to compart-mentalize the public from the private, the loser from the win-ner, and thus, when we consider what there is in ourselves that we might bring out to meet a need, we tally up short. We dis-count or dismiss what we see as "negatives" in ourselves, when they actually form many of the things we have to offer. Who better to help one alcoholic than a recovering alcoholic? Who else can grasp the pain of grief like another who has wailed in anguish? Who else can pave the way toward hope for an incest survivor like another survivor who has found her way?

Parenting challenges, failed relationships, territory recov-ered from addictions, financial losses, even convicted time served—*all* of the experiences in the *all* of you and me make up what we bring to a moment.

Only I could be my daughter's and son's mother. Only I can be my grandson's "Yia Yia." Only I can be married to

70

my husband, befriend my coworker who develops cancer in midlife, and invest who I have become where I am called to be.

What if I did what *I* could?

What if . . . I did what I **could**?
  What if I acted with what I have?
  What if I acted right where I am?
  What if I acted because it might
    matter?

11
What If . . .
I Did What I **Could**?

What if I took stock of my offerings and humbly but realistically grabbed hold of what I *could* do—and did it, without holding back? Even if it made little sense to those around me but all the sense in the world to God? How could I wholeheartedly let God love me and then love him back, if I did what I *could*?

"Leave her alone." That's what Jesus said to the room filled with criticism. In other words, "Quit bothering her." I turn the eyes of my imagination away from Jesus and look back at Mary, seeing her the way he sees her: earnest and pure; her action in the moment, beautiful.

I am struck by his command: "Leave her alone."
Her who?
Well, Mary, of course, but also *you*.
Dear one, leave *you* alone. Leave yourself alone. Quit

bothering the *her* that is *you*. Stop needling her, judging her, messing with her, being embarrassed by her. Don't tie her up in knots and make her all anxious and sweaty. Silence the stream of self-editing that tells her that she's not enough, that she's silly or worthless, that she has really bad ideas and is way out of line. Take your hands off her! Let her be!

That's pretty much what Jesus was saying—*is* saying now: "Let her bring what she possesses to me. Let her do what she *could*. Let her give, whatever it is."

That really makes me think.

What if I acted with what I have? What if I did what I could by giving what I think I can't live without? Could I live without another pair of black shoes? Could I make out a check for the same amount as my mortgage this month and invest in a school in India? I wonder . . .

Way back in my early working days, a young mom who worked in our office mentioned her family's struggle to make ends meet. It was a casual comment, made after she arrived one day and hung her stained coat on a hook in her office. Actually, it was more of a parka. It didn't really "work" for a dress coat, and in those days people wore dress coats to work.

Later that week, I was at the mall and noticed in a store window a beautiful pink coat. A wool, dress-length coat. I didn't even stop to think. I went into the store, bought the coat, and asked that it be shipped to our office. When it arrived, I didn't give myself away, but I did share her joy and surprise as she put on the coat and twirled in front of the rest of the staff.

I'm not telling on myself now to make you think I'm

cool. I'm telling you this now because in trying to make it clear that there is a sacrificial element to doing what you can, I want you to understand that the level of sacrifice doesn't have to take the action beyond what is possible. It was possible for me to pay for the pink coat. Yes, I had less left to spend for the rest of the month after doing so. But the expenditure was possible, and from that possibility, I made the investment.

Sometimes acting with what we have means we spend money. Other times we invest less tangible assets, such as love, time, or energy.

Linda, a friend who was dying of cancer, called me and in her usual forthright manner asked if I would handle her funeral service. By *handle*, she meant "speak at it." I'd never before "done" a funeral. I had been to them, of course, but I'd never offered more than a handful of wadded tissues as my role.

My friend's death was imminent. My schedule was packed. My only remaining parent was also hovering near death. My emotions were torn. My heart was heavy. And then I considered all the "but, but, buts" on my list and moved beyond them to the *could* in the question. *Could* I do this thing for her?

Instead of focusing on what I didn't have, I took inventory of me—of what I did have. Speaking at the service would cost me, but it was something I "had." Yes, I could.

After a long and rather exhausting week of meetings, I drove down to visit with Linda at her daughter's house. I had fretted over how I would honor her desires and give an accurate representation of her life. I hadn't known her except through work, and work is only one facet of a person's life. What in the world could I say to comfort her family and friends? When would I have time to compose some kind of message that would offer the hope they needed and deserved?

When I arrived, I was escorted to the living room, where Linda lay on a hospital bed. I scooted a chair close and leaned in as she spoke. Clearly in pain, she instructed me to speak from Hebrews 11:1: "Faith is the confidence that what we hope for will actually happen; it gives us assurance about things we cannot see."

At least I had a verse to work from, but now what?

I decided to go the question route. In interview style, I asked about her faith. What mattered to her and what didn't? When had she felt closest to God and when the furthest from him? What did she think heaven would be like, and how did she hold on to her hope for it?

After just twenty minutes, I had the message. Linda had preached it straight to me. All I had to do was write it down and get ready to speak it for her.

As Jesus had told the roomful of objectors, I had to "leave her alone." When I quit "bothering" myself, I discovered that my friend had already given me what *she* had and then *I* had it to give to others after her death.

What if I acted where I was? What if I did what I could in front of others? What if I held up a placard on Martin Luther King Jr. Day, even though I'm white? What if I sat and listened to my Buddhist friend—just listened? What if I met the eyes of the guy holding a cardboard sign at the intersection and then rolled down my window and handed him a bill?

Leave her alone. Quit bothering her, and discover what it means to do what I *could*, what you *could*.

When my son was going through a particularly tough spell, I considered my possible responses: silence or cajoling or retaliation? Prayer, for sure. My husband and I talked it over, and over, and over. Finally we determined that our best response was to err on the side of love. Again and again and again we chose to make sure that if our son ever looked back and questioned his choices, he would always see us forgiving, accepting, and embracing, not necessarily every choice he made, but his being, his personhood, his value on this planet, and his relationship to us as son.

Not everyone agreed with our approach. Some feared that we were too forgiving, that we didn't show enough tough love. In middle-of-the-night moments, we, too, wondered, *Is this what we could do? Is this what we should do?*

Leave her alone. Quit bothering her—me. Stop picking at my shortcomings, and instead, let myself be enough. I do what I *could*. I act with what I have. I act where I am. I act because it just might matter.

What if you did what you *could*? What if you quit bothering yourself with criticism and negative judgments? Tell the Judas voice in your head to leave your Mary alone. Now. "Let the children come to me. Don't stop them! For the Kingdom of God belongs to those who are like these children" (Luke 18:16).

What do you have? Maybe it's an open hand. Maybe it's ten extra minutes or fifty bucks. Or pet supplies left over after your dog died a while back. Whatever it is, act with it.

What neat thing might happen if you act on something that really matters? Go for it.

Imagine: *What might happen if I did what I could? How would I be changed? How would others be changed? How would Jesus be loved? How might others see the gospel—see Jesus—if I did what I could?*

What if I did what I could?
  As a result of my action, someone
    would be helped.
  As a result of my action, I would be
    better.
  As a result of my action, the world
    would be better.

What if I had a relationship that resulted
  in a response?

12
What If I Did What I Could?

What if I lived each day with the commitment to do what I could in that day, to know that I am loved by Jesus and to love him back?

I might schedule a meeting with the principal and press the school to provide the special services I know my child requires in order to be the best he can be.

I might go on bed rest during a difficult pregnancy in order to give the life inside of me a chance at life outside of me.

I might apologize to a friend I wounded.

I might resign from my job and make more time for my kids.

I might go back to work in order to provide more resources for my kids.

I might stay married.

I might forgive my mother.

I might forgive myself.

I might share my story—my struggle—my sins—in public so that others might hear that the God who has helped me can help them.

I might tithe more than makes sense but not more than I really can afford.

I might adopt a child.

I might bite my tongue instead of speaking.

I might vote.

I might make a cup of cocoa for my husband and take it to him while he watches TV. Not because he asked for it or because I need to be in his good graces. Just because.

I might get off the couch and go for a walk with my daughter.

What if I did what I could?

One Monday morning, a woman I didn't know well e-mailed me a prayer update about her young teen daughter who had become a mother. The woman ended her e-mail with a line that pretty much said she didn't have anyone to talk to. I stared at the words. I knew she worked near my office. I looked at the clock and scrolled through my calendar, where I found a free hour—just thirty minutes from then. I e-mailed her and asked her to meet for coffee. I had no idea what I'd say to her, but I drove to the coffee shop. I didn't become her sole support. I didn't promise to see her every week. I didn't fix her life. But I sat and listened. I did what I could.

Once, when my grandson was sleeping over at our house, I awoke in the middle of the night and climbed the stairs to check on him. The baby monitor had been quiet, but, of course, you never know for sure unless you check. As I stood looking at him, I noticed that his body seemed rigid, so I reached out my hand to pat his back—a big mistake for a woman who hoped to return to sleep that night. His little head shot up, and he looked at me. "Are you okay?" I asked.

"No, Yia Yia. My tummy hurts." After checking to see if he needed to throw up or something, I straightened back up. Then came the question: "Yia Yia, could you lie down with me?"

I thought about his question. *Could* I lie down with him? The question wasn't, "Will you stay up all night and never get any sleep yourself and never go back to your own bed?" No, the question was, "Could you lie down with me?"

Yes, I could. I climbed over the twin bed's safety bar and lay down with my grandson. I did what I could.

On another occasion, I stopped at Marshalls, looking for something to wear at my next speaking engagement. I found a skirt—shortish, blue and black and gray—that was just right to go with the top I'd already scored on sale. The skirt's price tag read $69.99. That was too much, and definitely more than I like to pay.

But I headed to the checkout anyway, where I plunked down the skirt along with several other clearance doodads I had found in the gift department.

"That'll be $32.95," the clerk announced.

"Did you get the skirt?" I asked.

"Yes," he answered.

"Did you take the security sensor off?"

He patted his hand over the garment. "Yes," he said.

"Okay." I swiped my credit card while a lump started in my throat. *Wow! That skirt was nearly seventy dollars, and I think I'm getting it for, like, nothing!* Then that thought slammed right up against the next one: *That's stealing, darling. That total can't be right. Say something.*

I'll wait and check the receipt—maybe it was more discounted than I thought.

Say something.

No.

Back and forth it went, the arguing in my head. I made it all the way out of the store and into my car, where I checked the receipt. The skirt wasn't listed. I was really hoping that the next thought—*It's too late to change now*—would kick in, but it didn't. I was hoping the arguing would stop once I got the skirt home and hung safely inside my closet. It didn't.

And then I remembered that I was planning to wear the skirt to a speaking engagement and that God would be completely justified in striking me dead on the spot if I stood and proclaimed his Word in a stolen skirt! I would just have to go back to the store the next day and fess up—which I did.

It is *so* miserable to hand your credit card and receipt over to a clerk who couldn't care less, endure her incredulous stare, and know that $69.99 is being added to your card balance.

The clerk wasn't at all impressed that I had returned to make things right. If I had been in her position, I would have called the manager and reported over the loudspeaker the high level of integrity my customer had. I might even have given her a gift card good for twenty-five dollars toward a future purchase.

I honestly confess that I *so* didn't want to do what I could in that situation. But I did it.

What if every day I did what I could? What if every day I did what I could because I'm so convinced that Jesus loves me? What if the way I love Jesus in return for his loving me is to do what I could? What if the way Jesus shows the gospel to this world is sometimes through *me*—doing what I could?

As we clearly see in the story of Mary of Bethany, a relationship with Jesus results in a response. But just as Mary had no control over how her action would be received by those who observed it, I'm not able to control others' reactions to my response.

I might be rejected. Others might decide that my doing what I could is excessive, wasteful, inappropriate, or an all-about-me attempt to get attention.

I might be ridiculed: Ha! Who do you think you are with all this "she did what she could" stuff?

I might be honored.

I might make Jesus smile. I might demonstrate my extreme gratitude for his loving me by loving him back in a moment when my action means something to his people and his planet and, therefore, to him.

I'm not responsible for the response to my response. I'm just invited to respond. When I do what I could, I tell the Good News of the gospel to the world around me. A relationship that results in a response is a beautiful thing. I am changed, and I change my world. *When I do what I could.*

PART 3

What If We Did What We Could?

What if . . . **we** did what **we** could?

What could we all accomplish if all of us did what we could?

What could we do together that we couldn't do alone?

What if I did what I could and you did what you could and then we did what we could?

13
What If . . .
We Did What *We* Could?

We who? You plus me equals we.

What if *we* did what *we* could? What could we do together that we couldn't do alone?

The answer to that question isn't so hard: We could do lots. I can do only what I can do: reach out to the folks on my street, at my job, in my marketplace, in my kids' school, and in my church with my skills and my story and my money and my perspective. If I did what I could, I could do quite a bit. But I couldn't do nearly as much as if together *we* did what *we* could.

Think about it! Imagine what could happen if we added just what I could do to what you could do. And then you and I added a few more of us: people in the book club, the office, the church, the neighborhood, my city, your city, the state.

Five plus 15 plus 50 plus 100 plus 1,000 plus 5,000 plus 10,000 plus 50,000 plus 100,000 plus 1,000,000.

What if *we* did what *we* could?

What could we *all* accomplish if each one of us did what she could and then *we* added all these efforts together? This is the body of Christ in action—uniquely called to both an individual and a corporate investment of who *we* are.

My friend Debbie loves stirring up interest in global issues, believing that God's passion is for the world—all of it. She wants to get Christians involved with world issues. Her concern is both personal and planetwide. So she talks to anyone who will listen and offers to strategize with those people to connect others in conversations. Her dream is to set up ongoing groups in churches for prayer, discussion, and eventually involvement. What if there were a Debbie in every church?

Tracy believes that God gave the earth to people to enjoy and to steward. Only a few months after she was hired, she asked the president of her company for permission to spearhead a recycling program. Today the company has shredders for paper and recycling bins for plastic, cardboard, glass, and other items stationed all around the office building. What if there were a Tracy in every office?

Another friend, Debbie, and her husband, Rick, heard about women in undeveloped countries who have no supplies for attending to the most basic daily responsibilities, like washing clothes and preparing food. Then they discovered Global Action, a ministry organization that sends Buckets of Love to impoverished women. The actual buckets are filled with basic supplies such as soap, washcloths, toothbrushes and toothpaste, tape, twine, simple toys for children, and other necessary items, fourteen in all. Rick and Debbie funded several buckets. And then they replaced company-client Christmas gifts with notifications that they were funding more. What if there were a Rick and Debbie in every business?

Doug and Cindy have a passion for healthy marriages. As expatriates, they spent nearly a decade in the United Kingdom, where they gathered friends at a local pub every week to dive into discussions about how marriage really works. Now back in the States, they're recreating this effort in a local bar. Couples are coming—and growing in their relationships. What if there were a Doug and Cindy in every bar?

One. 15. 60. 150. 3,200. 10,683. What could we *all* accomplish if one or two or three of us did what we could and then *we* added our efforts together?

> *Amor mundi* [love for the world] [is] our being quickened to a divine but painful compassion for the world. . . . And it is *amor mundi* that compels millions of ordinary folk like you and me to minister life in Christ's good name to our neighbor, our *nigh-bor*: "the person who is near us."[1]
> —Richard Foster

SDWSC. We decide the concept is exciting and highly motivational. We can hardly wait to get started. And so, full of good intentions, we dive in and are SDWSC-ing away when *bam!*—we're blindsided by criticism. We get grief instead of support.

Have you ever run into people who demand that you

believe everything the way they believe it or you can't be part of their "we"? Have you ever experienced what it feels like to be excluded from the great Christian "we"?

Mary nearly was. A room full of followers collectively gasped at her action and then troubled her to the point of rejection. If the folks at that dinner party had had their way, Mary would never have acted at all, her gift of anointing Jesus' body before his death scuttled before it could even get away from the dock. But Jesus interceded. He pronounced her action beautiful and paired it with the preaching of the Good News for all time.

How often we use our *we* to cripple the body of Christ rather than to release God's power in us and through us: Believe the way *we* believe. Attack the "enemies" *we* attack. Parent the way *we* parent. Support the causes *we* support. Be like us. Be *we*, not them. They do things *we* don't do. They believe things *we* don't believe. They go places *we* don't go. They hang out with other "thems." They can't be *we*.

But just as Jesus interceded for Mary, he intercedes for us. A relationship with Jesus results in a response. When *we* are loved, *we* can live loved.

> Most people in my generation have grown up believing that a Christian is defined by what he or she doesn't do. We are beginning to understand that a Christian is better defined as someone who does certain behaviors that are reflective of love, mercy, justice, and compassion.
> —Jena Nardella, executive director, Blood:Water Mission, Nashville, Tennessee

Occasionally in the ministry world, ultimatums are delivered, muscles are flexed, and threats are made: Match our political agenda, or you're out. Parrot our passions, or you won't sell books in our circles. Say the words the way we say them, or you won't have a speaking platform with us.

What ministry leader hasn't experienced the pain of diminished Kingdom impact because some powerful part of the Kingdom decided that leader wasn't "we"? It's very common.

I once bumped up against a ministry giant in just such a scenario. When our board members received an ultimatum, they refused to bend to it. Our board believed that the other ministry's mission—while Kingdom-centered and valid—wasn't our mission. Strong convictions held that taking on their mission as ours would actually hamper our efforts to accomplish what God had called us to do. When the ministry giant withdrew its support, we lost out big-time. It hurt—corporately and personally. The wound was painful, heart-heavy, and hard to bear.

Notice all the *we*'s and *they*'s in this language. Isn't this where such thinking leads us? To focus on opposing one another rather than on fulfilling our common Kingdom purposes?

During that difficult season, an image came to me that helped me to see the Kingdom of God as a whole posse of individuals who together form a varied and multifaceted community. I saw thousands of individual believers, standing side by side in a circle and facing *out* rather than each other. As people looked out to the Kingdom cause directly in front of them—their slice of the whole Kingdom effort—they could see only those people who stood next to them.

As they looked to the right and to the left, they were strengthened by the sight of the ones they saw fighting beside them. But from where they stood, they concluded that those fighting side by side with them were the *only* ones fighting for the Kingdom. Aside from their comrades beside them, they believed they were alone in the battle. Anyone who wasn't standing right beside them was not fighting the cause to which they were committed and, in fact, was not fighting for the Kingdom at all.

As I thought about that image, I was struck by the fact that if we were just to turn and look over our shoulders— all of us—we would see that none of us is alone. Thousands and millions of brothers and sisters are standing along the Kingdom circle, addressing *their* particular issues and causes in their slice of the Kingdom, their part of the overall *we*.

In order to understand both the uniqueness and the magnitude of Kingdom calls, we have to look beyond those at our sides. We have to look over our shoulders and take in all those who "have our backs." Only then can we begin to understand the great communal effort that is taking place as one after another *we* respond to our own relationships with Jesus.

> While the power of one is impressive, the power of community is awe-inspiring.
> —Gloria Luna, director, Office of Social Advocacy, Catholic Charities, Archdiocese of Miami, Florida

Let me be clear. The essentials regarding the tenets of our faith in Christ—our beliefs about what makes Christianity Christianity and Christians Christians—are the foundation of *we*. But the specifics related to how each of us actively responds to our relationship with Jesus can vary from individual to individual and from call to call. Christ calls us into a relationship with him. He is the source of our offerings, of our actions. Each relationship results in a response that will be personal and contextualized in the world in which *we* live.

SDWSC is a powerful response to a relationship of healing that Jesus paired with the gospel for all time. She did what she could.

> The greatest social need in the world today is not HIV/ AIDS outreach. It's not hunger. It's not global warming. Not ending poverty or eliminating malaria or tuberculosis. Not clean water. Not racial reconciliation. Not sexual trafficking. Not abortion. And it's not peace in the Middle East, and not even world peace. . . . None of [our] good works—nay, great works—deal with the most profound social problem facing humankind. That social problem is alienation from God.[2]

A relationship with Jesus is radical and transformational. We are changed by this relationship. And when we are changed, we want to change our world. Our relationship results in a response.

> There are two conversions in life: coming to Christ and then reformation—doing something about it.[3]
> —Rick Warren

All of us who sit at the feet of Jesus and are changed by his love are destined—no, *called*—to move on to the second conversion of expressing our faith in our actions. To do what we could.

> Caring for the suffering is not optional, and it's not for just a certain group of people. It should be a hallmark of our faith.[4]
> —Kay Warren

It's vital that each one of us do what *we* individually could. It is also vital that *we* do what *we* could together and that we respect how others do what they could so that *we* are all doing what *we* could. We don't have to be the same to be *we*. We don't have to agree with each other's finer points of theology to serve a meal to the hungry. We don't have to tackle the same issues at the same moment with the same verbiage in order for God's Kingdom to advance. In fact, in many cases we will have less impact if we all do the same thing than we would if we each did what we could alone and then all our efforts were added to a communal *we*.

What could we all accomplish if each one of us did what we could? I might minister to moms. You might stand against abuse. He feeds the hungry. She works for justice. They advocate for the homeless. Together, we might change the world. Many acts. One we.

> The human body has many parts, but the many parts make up one whole body. . . . If the whole body were an eye, how would you hear? Or if your whole body were an ear, how

would you smell anything? But our bodies have many parts, and God has put each part just where he wants it. How strange a body would be if it had only one part! Yes, there are many parts, but only one body.

—1 Corinthians 12:12, 17-20

She did what she could. One girl entered a relationship with Jesus, and because a relationship with Jesus results in a response, she did what she could. She lived loved. Jesus invites us to do the same. He beckons us to a relationship with him, a relationship that results in a response, an action. Going. Doing. Giving. Loving. When we know Jesus and are known by him, we can live loved—all of us. Individually and together. You. And me. *We.*

What if . . . *we* did what *we* could?

What if we did what we could?
How would we change?
How would we change our world?

14
What If We Did
What We Could?

What if I did what I could and you did what you could and
then we did what we could—all of us?

There are days when it all seems so impossible, like the
evening I watched NBC *Nightly News* with Brian Williams and
learned of the plight of mentally retarded adults in Serbia.

Most of us care, remember? We really do. We care about
our own lives, for sure, and also about the lives of those around
us. We care about poverty and injustice, about orphans and
the sick. We care about the folks who live and work alongside
us and about what happens in their families and their hearts
and their heads.

We care. But too often we stop there because we think
that in order for it to count, to make a difference that matters,
we have to do something *big*. Or *everything* we could do. Or
something no one else has done.

But as we've seen, that's not true. Five letters representing five words make a world of difference. *SDWSC*. She did what she could.

From the online World Vision HIV/AIDS exhibit, I learned that thirty-three million people are living with HIV.[1] Six thousand people die every day. Whole generations have been lost. As I listened to Gary Haugen of the International Justice Mission, I discovered that twenty-seven million people are living in slavery and two million children exist in forced prostitution. Twenty-four thousand children die of starvation *every day*.

How can this be?

It's too much. Most of us do well just to get through to dinner, bath time, and bedtime. We hold the future in our hands as we rock our babies, love our little ones, nurture them with everything we have, and pray they will grow to be healthy, contributing, God-loving adults.

That's a lot—isn't it?

Yes, it's a lot. But what if each of us, you and I, did what we could? How might our actions be paired with the gospel so that people could see Jesus?

What if . . .

* * *

Karen lost one of her six children. Perhaps a better way to put it is that if all of Karen's children had lived, she would have six rather than five. Or would she even have the five without the loss of the one?

First came a son. Then another son, who lived only a few hours. Then a healthy boy. Then a gorgeous baby girl. Throughout the journey into—and out of—parenthood, a desire to adopt had grown in Karen's and her husband's hearts.

As the years passed, Karen continued to yearn for children she didn't know, had never seen. At first she and her husband were drawn to Brazil and journeyed there to investigate the possibility of adoption. But they found the doors closed, and they obligingly turned toward home, only to find their hearts leapfrogging across the Atlantic toward Africa. They researched, prayed, waited, worked, mobilized to act in response to the HIV/AIDS pandemic. Fighting and finally winning, they adopted a brother and sister from Ethiopia.

Karen and her husband weren't completely selfless souls who, Mother Teresa–like, wanted to care for the orphans of the world. They were a couple in need of children to complete their family.

Three children instead of four led to five children instead of three. They did what they could.

* * *

Evan and his wife were returning from a weekend getaway. It had been fun—a treat, in fact. They had preboarded the plane and settled into their traveling postures: Evan at work on his laptop and his wife reading a magazine.

He looked up when her elbow dug into his side.

"Keep an eye on him!" she whispered, as an old, unshaven man wearing a plaid flannel shirt and sweatpants slid into the seat across the aisle from them and next to a young teenage girl. With the smell of alcohol heavy about him, he clutched a plastic shopping bag with a recognizable logo. Somehow Evan doubted that the man shopped there.

Everything seemed okay until midflight and a few drinks later, when the old man reached down unsteadily for his shopping bag and Evan caught sight of its contents: a plastic urinal.

Uh-oh.

"Sir." Evan leaned across the aisle. "You really can't use that here."

"Well, I can't make it to the lavatory. I'll fall on my a--." The man belched.

Evan closed his laptop, handed it to his wife, raised his tray table, unfastened his seat belt, and stood up. He leaned down and helped the man unbuckle his own seat belt and ushered him, weaving up the aisle, to the lavatory, where he helped him inside and then kept an eye out through the crack in the door until the old man was ready to return to his seat.

He did what he could.

● ● ●

Angel had been a leader in her MOPS group for more than a decade. She had a heart for the underdog: teen moms, moms on welfare, moms who lacked transportation, single moms, working moms, moms who were new in the community. Angel wanted all of them—every one of them—to discover the hope and help they could find in a relationship with Jesus.

She'd discovered him, herself, while in some pretty needy messes.

Years into various renditions of MOPS, Angel looked around and asked herself, *Where else on earth are there mothers?* To Angel's surprise, God directed her to consider moms who were incarcerated.

She contacted the sheriff at the Orange County correctional facility, near where she lived. She discovered that within the inmate population there was a large concentration of moms of young children. She asked for, and was granted, the opportunity to start a MOPS group for these women. And week after week, Angel and her team of helpers check their purses and belongings on one side of a reinforced door and then walk through it to bring hope and healing to the moms on the other side.

She did what she could.

● ● ●

Joanna needed volunteer hours for her high school service record. As an underclassman she chose ESL—English as a Second Language—and began tutoring women from Burma/Myanmar and Nigeria.

One woman told her, "I thought all Americans had guns. I was wrong. You've shown me love." What began as a high-school graduation requirement grabbed at Joanna's heart and became a passion.

As she prepared to finish her senior year, it became important to her that this program continue—and that the impact on her peers who would participate would be as great as it had been on her. So Joanna spent the remaining months of high school finding a replacement for herself and was able to link a local graduate equivalency diploma (GED) program to the ESL classes as well. She hadn't thought her volunteering would matter so very much—until it did.

So she did what she could.

● ● ●

After what seemed a "routine" hysterectomy, Jane discovered she had cancer, an aggressive, deadly cancer of the blood. Vibrant Jane, in her early sixties, was still teaching kindergarten at the private school she'd helped found more than twenty years earlier. Her daughter was about to be married, her oldest son was about to make her a grandmother, and suddenly—Jane was dying.

Dying? No way!

After exhaustive and exhausting tests, Jane and her family came to terms with the poor prognosis, and Jane began treatment to prolong her life. Their goal was for Jane to attend her daughter's wedding and hold her grandbaby.

Because Jane needed emergency treatment to stem internal bleeding, she missed the wedding celebration. But her daughter and the entire wedding party brought the real wedding to Jane, the bride and groom exchanging vows in the hospital chapel before returning to the site of the wedding and the reception.

Then, on schedule, Jane welcomed her first grandson, joyed beyond belief at his arrival.

In an unexpected season when good things happened only rarely, Jane received a treatment that extended her life. Over a year past her diagnosis, Jane made her bed each morning and fixed dinner each night. She drove to the school she'd founded and volunteered two days a week because, she said, "The hardest part about cancer is having your purpose taken away."

Jane still had cancer. The prognosis was that she would have an indefinite but likely short period of time for productive contribution. So Jane invested.

She did what she could.

● ● ●

Lee worried about her son: single, young, still in school, and bumping along in and out of sobriety. She longed to see him whole—no, healed. Her own journey to recovery had taught her that providing that healing for her son was beyond her own ability. No, his healing would require a journey of his own.

Just then, he stumbled and fell again. As Lee stepped back out of his path, grieving his self-destruction, she wondered just how her efforts could ever make a difference. Three months later, as her son was leaving the court appointment where he'd faced some legal consequences for his drinking, he called her. He was admitting himself to an inpatient treatment facility. Would she keep his dog—his intimidating, ninety-pound, eighteen-month-old dog—during the same weeks her kitchen and family-room floors were undergoing reconstruction and she was also caring for her four-year-old grandson?

She would. She did what she could.

● ● ●

Every Friday at noon, Dennis, Sharon, and Bill met for a quick bite to eat and then set to work. Dennis took the left side of the sanctuary, Sharon took the middle, and Bill took the right. Methodically, sometimes painfully, they moved from row to row to row, checking the pencils and the prayer cards.

They replaced the pencils that had broken points with sharpened ones. If the prayer cards had been doodled on, they were thrown away, and new ones were put in their place.

To some, this weekly ritual might seem insignificant, even silly. But to this faithful trio, it meant volumes. They knew that each Sunday morning, someone—many someones—would reach for a pencil and a prayer card and jot down a need. They knew this because after the Sunday services, the same trio gathered the cards and handed them to the deacons for action.

They did what they could.

● ● ●

Valerie took her husband's place on a trip to Kenya scheduled for various high-ranking ministry leaders in their association. She had no idea what she'd discover, but sensing it would be a life-altering journey, she armed herself with a journal and an open spirit and prepared to record every element of the trip. Or so she thought. Much of the time her heart simply broke open and leaked in a trail of emotion.

When she returned, she was changed. She simply could not *not* act. Each day she awoke to images of cows. If she could send money for cows to the woman who had become wedged in Valerie's soul, that woman could not only survive but also begin to make her way toward a life of her own. But Valerie didn't have money. She was a simple American woman trying to make her way as well.

Little by little, the realization dawned on Valerie that she could do a lot—a little at a time. At the grocery store, she asked that the savings from using her frequent-customer card be given to her in cash rather than deducted from her bill. Then she stashed away that amount each week. She made a commitment to avoid buying new clothing for a period of time and pocketed that savings as well. She clipped coupons and shopped at flea markets for gifts. Eventually, when she finally counted out her savings, she found she had enough to buy a starter herd of cattle for her new African friend.

She did what she could.

• • •

He had captured her heart with just a smile, a dimpled, joy-filled, sunburst of a grin. Sharon had never before loved with such abandon—she abandoned her to-do list, her carefully scheduled workday, even her favorite TV programs. She left it all, over and over, for this little three-year-old wonder.

When her daughter had revealed her pregnancy, Sharon had been hesitant. Was this young woman ready to mother? Was Sharon herself old enough to be "grandmotherly"? Goodness!

Over the years, Sharon's resolve to keep her grandson at a bit of a distance had evaporated. She fairly *ate him up*, so delightful was the lavish yumminess he brought to her life. And yet she wondered: Would her daughter teach him the simple prayers so precious to childhood? Would she teach him about God, about his own need for faith?

And then the idea came to her. She could teach him *herself* if it was okay with her daughter—and it was! So she picked up a couple of books about Jesus, and on her grandson's next visit, she tentatively opened them with him. He loved them! She bowed her head and held his hands in hers over his dinner of chicken nuggets and fries and prayed out loud, inviting him to repeat after her. He did! She buckled him into a car seat and took him with her to church. He loved it! She taught him—bit by bit—about *her* love for Jesus and Jesus' love for *him*.

She did what she could.

● ● ●

Judy had prayed for her prodigal son, Josh, for two years before she shared her pain with a friend. Then, in just minutes, she discovered how very *not* alone she was in her struggle. Serving in an international ministry with her husband, she heard story after story of parents' hearts broken over their prodigal children.

So Judy launched a Web-based prayer effort that drew together parents from every part of the world to pray their wayward ones home.

She did what she could.

● ● ●

Rob had been in the consulting business for a long time, maybe even forty years. He helped with executive- and senior-level searches. He knew people *everywhere*. Now, just months after retiring from his full-time role, he found himself seated next to a woman in a transition from CEO to goodness-knows-what. He'd heard some version of her story many times, along with the tentative, exploratory questions she mulled over regarding what might be next.

He knew he could help. Although he didn't have specific

answers about what her next steps should be, he was well acquainted with the questions she asked—and with the process ahead of her as she sought the answers she needed.

Reaching for his wallet, he found one remaining—rather dog-eared—business card. As he held it out to his seatmate, he invited her to call him for a free consultation.

He did what he could.

● ● ●

Beth hoisted the box of Easter decorations onto her kitchen counter. Over the years she had collected five or six different styles of plastic eggs, with a dozen in each set. They were great for the egg hunts and allowed adults and children of all ages to run about crazily in search of a color-coded treasure.

As she laid out the eggs and matched them to her kids and grandkids, she realized she had an extra set. What to do?

Then Ericka, her nail tech, popped into her mind. Beth didn't know her well, but the last time she had her nails done, Ericka had shared her disappointment over the fact that the deal had fallen through on the house she'd hoped to buy for herself and her two-year-old son. And the fact that the guy she'd been seeing had turned out to be—well, she wasn't seeing him anymore.

Beth wondered what Ericka and her little boy were doing on Easter Sunday. She had Ericka's cell-phone number. She could dial it and invite them to come for the afternoon.

She did what she could.

● ● ●

She Did What She Could. Five words that have changed my life.

Have they changed yours?

It's time to put down the book and pick up the challenge. You don't have to start another nonprofit (though, of course, you could). You don't even have to get off the couch. Just pick up the phone.

You. Act out of who *you* are.

Do. Don't just think about it. *Do* it.

What. What's your *what*? What keeps you from doing your *what*?

You. The moment is uniquely before *you*. Act out of who you are now and the you God is making you to be.

Could. The opportunity is here, now. It matters. Do what you can do.

A relationship with Jesus results in a response. So go ahead. Get out there and live loved.

SDWSC.

Afterword

The SDWSC stories in this book are real stories. In some, the names and certain details have been changed to preserve anonymity. Other stories remain unchanged and have been included with permission.

The purpose of these stories is to demonstrate just how simple and yet profound an SDWSC moment can be.

As these five letters, representing five words, take root in your heart, you may discover one—or many—SDWSC stories of your own. When you do, please consider sharing them at www.shedidwhatshecould.com.

A relationship with Jesus results in a response.

Notes

Chapter 3: She Did *What* She Could

1. J. D. Douglas (revising ed.) and Merrill C. Tenney (general ed.), *The New International Dictionary of the Bible, Pictorial Edition* (Grand Rapids: Zondervan, 1987), 804.

Chapter 4: She Did What *She* Could

1. William Barclay, *The Gospel of Mark* (Philadelphia: Westminster Press, 1975), 326.

Chapter 13: What If . . . *We* Did What *We* Could?

1. Richard Foster, "Spiritual Formation Agenda," *Christianity Today* (January 2009): 33.
2. "The Greatest Social Need," editorial in *Christianity Today* (January 2009): 18.
3. Rick Warren, as quoted by Bill Hybels.
4. Kay Warren, "My Heart Has Been Broken by the Suffering of AIDS," interview by Connie Willems, *Discipleship Journal* (March/April 2008): 54.

Chapter 14: What If We Did What We Could?

1. See http://www.worldvisionexperience.org/learn_crisis.asp, accessed May 20, 2009.

About the Author

Elisa Morgan is one of today's most sought-after authors, speakers, and leaders. She is the author of more than fifteen books on mothering, spiritual formation, and evangelism and is the publisher of *FullFill* (www.fullfill.org), a leadership-development resource for women of all ages, stages, and callings.

For twenty years, Elisa served as CEO of MOPS (Mothers of Preschoolers) International. Under her leadership, MOPS grew from 350 local groups to more than 4,000 groups throughout the United States and in thirty other countries and having an impact on more than 100,000 moms every year. In 2009, Elisa moved from her role as CEO to that of president emerita.

Educated at the University of Texas, where she earned a bachelor's degree in psychology, and at Denver Seminary, where she earned a Master's of Divinity, she has served on the board of ECFA (Evangelical Council for Financial Accountability) and offers one of the few female voices in professional Christian leadership today.

Elisa is married to Evan (vice-president of strategic development for RBC Ministries—known internationally for Our Daily Bread—and founder of christiancourses.com). They have two grown children and one grandchild and live in Centennial, Colorado.